IS AMERICAN CHRISTIANITY ANTICHRIST?

THE ROOT CAUSE OF HATE IN AMERICA

Carolyn S. Byars, MDiv

Copyright © 2022 Carolyn S. Byars
All rights reserved.
ISBN: 979-8-35255-931-4

CSByars Publishing

Scripture quotations, unless otherwise noted, are from the Amplified Bible (AMP) from Biblegateway.com.

DEDICATION

To the Body of Christ, the authentic followers of Jesus Christ in America and all around the world.

ACKNOWLEDGMENTS

I have learned in life that when God gives us an assignment, He always provides everything we need to get His work done. I am eternally grateful to God for the wonderful people He placed in my life who were willing to read (and re-read) my writings and provide me with their critical feedback, wisdom, and insight.

Thank you, Rev. Dr. Judy Fisher, my pastor, spiritual mentor, and advisor, for being the first person to encourage me to write this book after reading my treatise, *American Christianity vs Authentic Christianity*. Thank you, Rev. Percy L. Myers, for faithfully reading and critiquing every piece I wrote with such amazing precision and objectivity during my two-year book writing journey. Thank you, Dr. Curtis Dodson, for providing such a comprehensive description of the antichrist spirit. Your decades of scholarly research on eschatology and teaching the book of Revelation is a gift to the Body of Christ. Thank you, Elaine Todd, Ph.D. for reviewing my manuscript and providing guidance on the publishing process. Thank you, Shirley Turner, Ph.D., author, and English professor for taking time from your very demanding schedule to edit my manuscript. Thank you to my very dear friends Charlotte Sewell, Betty Shaw, and Rev. Marline Gamble, for being my prayer partners and spiritual cheerleaders! A post-mortem thank-you to the late Bishop George D. McKinney, Ph.D. for encouraging me to submit my treatise for publication.

CONTENTS

Foreword 2
Introduction 5
1 American Christianity vs Authentic Christianity 7
2 Open Letter to Christian Churches in America 18
3 Is American Christianity Antichrist? – Where is the Love? 25
4 Is American Christianity Antichrist? – The Most Divided Hour in America 33
5 Is American Christianity Antichrist? – White Supremacy Continues to Reign 43
6 Is a Christian Nation a Possibility? 51
7 Christian and Conservative 66
8 The Antichrist Spirit 76
9 Is American Christianity Antichrist? – Conclusion 87
Bibliography 94

Foreword

While it may seem a bit unusual to start a book's foreword this way, I am inclined to warn readers to hold on to their seats as the author takes them on a journey that will make them question their faith and their sanity. At times, you will feel as if you are being led into the world of fake news and clandestine plots to undermine your faith in Jesus Christ. The African American spiritual, "Sometimes, I Feel Like a Motherless Child", comes to mind as I struggle to write this foreword in such a way that will invite the reader to experience a journey into the world of politics and the right-wing Christians who brandish guns and weapons of destruction when they "prayerfully" terrorized our US Capitol January 6, 2021. And yet, they think they were doing God's will to "make America better".

The author of this gripping book is a seminary-trained ordained minister. Carolyn grew up in one of the largest Pentecostal churches in the world. She is keenly aware of the language of the church, its rites, rituals, conventions, convocations, doctrines, and dogma. Her father was a pastor and her mother was a master teacher both in the public school system and the church world.

For many years, the author fellowshipped with different church congregations, and her personal experience in various church traditions provided ample exposure to what she writes about in this book. Her spiritual eyes were awakened to extremist ideologies, racism, and contempt toward people of color. She is well-acquainted with churches of every size, racial makeup, and leadership style. It is from her personal experience that this book began to take shape as she decided to do research to find out "what's going on" as she states in her introduction.

Many readers may become disturbed or angry while reading

this treatise as it reveals in very clear terms, just what is going on. She carefully and clearly lays out the issues that confront the Christian church in America. Readers will not be able to deny what is going on and will have to confront the truth about the active role that American Christianity plays in the perpetuation of racism and hate-mongering. These two evils precipitate the outrageous display of the antichrist spirit among American Evangelicals, Christian nationalists, and right-wing political and social groups. The author brilliantly discloses how the founding fathers were all about gaining economic power and control by forcing slavery upon Africans and thus justified the creation and practice of a new religion she identifies as American Christianity.

The beauty of this book is that it lays out for the reader every scripture that substantiates her viewpoints. The scriptures are provided for the readers to examine immediately! She reveals every breach of God's Word concerning the apostate Church uncovered by her research to answer the question, "Is American Christianity Antichrist?" Thus, the reader has to face their own prejudices and then choose to deal with them appropriately by repenting and asking the Lord to forgive them for their failure to live as Christians motivated by love.

You may ask why I have so much faith in Carolyn's research and work. I have had the pleasure of knowing her in Christian fellowship for decades. I also had the distinct pleasure of ordaining her into ministry in the Thurman Chapel at Howard University School of Divinity. She demonstrated her commitment to ministry and her life bore testimony of her fidelity and Christian living. I am happy to say that as her pastor, I encouraged her to write this book and I have supported its publication every step of the way.

This book verifies that the author has been given marching orders by God to go forth and to declare scripturally what is going on in our world, particularly in the Church world. Every believer and non-believer need to read this book...this work of art... that was birthed under the auspices of the Holy Spirit.

It is food for the soul and a light unto our feet. It rings a warning bell for the true Christians of today. At the same time, it bears the truth and shows the way of true repentance to those who have lost their way so that they may become acquainted with the true and living God! You will not regret your investment in the truth about how to make America Great! Buy the book and pass it on! You can help make America great by understanding the root cause of hatred and taking action, motivated by love, to repair the breach in American society with and by the Word of God.

Bishop Judy Ann Fisher

Introduction

As you listen to and watch news reports daily, have you asked yourself, "What is behind the violence and divisiveness among Americans today?" Why are Americans so captivated by lies and extremist ideologies? Why are people who claim to be Christians spewing such hatred towards those who do not conform to "Christian morals and values?" Why is there such contempt towards people of color and non-Anglo cultures and ethnicities? How is it possible that a nation that proudly proclaims to be the "greatest nation on earth" continues to suffer the "plague of gun violence" more than any other nation in the world? What is the rationale for Christians opposing abortions and at the same time supporting laws that allow innocent children to be murdered en masse by gun violence? Is it rooted in politics? Is it fueled by religious bigotry?

Over 50 years ago the late Marvin Gaye prophetically wrote and sang "What's Going On?" Sadly, this song is just as meaningful in 2022 as it was those many years ago. My journey in seeking answers to "What's going on?" began with my writing the treatise *American Christianity vs Authentic Christianity* in response to the murder of George Floyd in May 2020. I had no idea that the treatise would evolve into a book with such a controversial title, *Is American Christianity Antichrist? The Root Cause of Hate in America*. Written over two years, beginning with my treatise, this book became a collection of essays and sermons focused specifically on Christianity in America. For centuries Christians have pointed an accusing finger at secularism as the cause of evil in our society. However, as I conducted my research on the ideologies of American Christianity and Christian nationalism, I kept asking myself over and over again, "Where is the love of Jesus in all the vitriol coming out of the mouths of Americans who identify as Christians?"

The premise for writing this book is to expose how American

Christianity aids and abets the tactics of the antichrist spirit to steal, kill, and destroy our nation by perverting and distorting the true message of Jesus Christ. Contrary to popular belief, the US Constitution can never preempt the Word of God. Man-made laws have no power to make anyone Christian. However, being in a relationship with Jesus and following His teachings, we are empowered to resist and thwart the enemy in this antichrist-infected world system.

I desire that as you read this collection of sermons and essays, you will be inspired to spend time in self-reflection and assess your relationship with God. Guided by the Holy Spirit, you will make the corrections in your attitude and treatment of others that truly honor God. Romans 12:21 assures authentic followers of Jesus that we are not to be overcome *and* conquered by evil, but we can overcome evil with good.

The only hope for America is Jesus! This is an imperfect world populated with imperfect people. But as authentic followers of Jesus, we can be positive influencers and change agents in America and the world at large when we exemplify and **SHARE THE LOVE Of JESUS!**

1 American Christianity vs Authentic Christianity

May 2020

Right now, I am overwhelmed with anger, grief, and despair concerning the treatment of Americans of African descent, namely George Floyd, Christian Cooper, Ahmaud Arbery, and Breonna Taylor. Many ascribe these heinous crimes against people of color to racism. However, the Word of God defines such ungodly behavior as hate. Every disciple of Jesus Christ knows where hate originates. But how are we to respond to hate? Jesus instructs us in Luke 7:27 "But I say to you who hear [Me and pay attention to My words]: Love [that is, unselfishly seek the best or higher good for] your enemies, [make it a practice to] do good to those who hate you…" Sadly the only one of these four individuals to survive was Mr. Cooper. A woman Mr. Cooper encountered in New York Central Park called 911 falsely accusing him of threatening her. Later he expressed how uncomfortable he felt with the amount of backlash the woman received, including losing her job. Even though the woman was attempting to set him up to be killed by the police, Mr. Cooper chose to extend grace rather than revenge upon her. Wow!

As Christians, our first response to any crisis should always be prayer. However, Jesus admonished the disciples to "watch and pray" (Mark 14:38). I believe that even though we are fervently praying, we are not watching. Watch means to be on the alert, vigilant, and on the lookout for any threats of evil. We must be alert and vigilant to take action to wipe out the evil of hatred with the love of God whenever it rears its ugly head.

Why is it that living in America is so dangerous for people of color in general and African American males in particular? I have concluded that it is because many Americans believe that America is fundamentally a Christian nation. But the history of America taught in schools for centuries is a fairy tale. I will admit that I once was duped by the narrative that this nation was established solely to give Christians freedom to practice their Christian faith. The truth is that America came about from countless acts of terrorism perpetrated by European explorers. The explorers did not "discover" America but rather exploited the people and the land already inhabited by the native nations. A few years ago, I read an article in the Washington Post by Catherine Rampell titled "Founding Fathers, Trashing Immigrants". To my dismay I discovered the following statement made by Benjamin Franklin, "Why increase the Sons of *Africa*, by planting them in *America*, where we have so fair an Opportunity, by excluding all Blacks and Tawneys, of increasing the lovely White and Red?" I am convinced that the religion of the Founding Fathers was all about gaining economic power and control by forcing slavery upon Africans. This resulted in the creation and practice of a new religion which I choose to call "American Christianity". In my response to this, I am compelled to quote Isaiah 58:1 "Cry aloud, do not hold back; Lift up your voice like a trumpet, And declare to My people their transgression".

I identified twelve tenets of American Christianity and contrasted them with Authentic Christianity in the following table.

American Christianity Tenets	Authentic Christianity
1. Believe that America is a Christian nation by law and practice.	Know that being a Christian is the result of an individual (not a nation) choosing to become a disciple of Jesus Christ and live their lives following His teachings. *"Then Jesus said to his disciples, "Whoever wants to be my disciple must*

	deny themselves and take up their cross and follow me." Matt 16:24
2. Believe that the US Constitution entitles them to certain freedoms, rights, and privileges.	Know that freedom is gained from God's Truth and not the Constitution. The writers of the Constitution were only focused on obtaining freedom for white male landowners. Freedom for women, natives, and enslaved Africans was not considered at all by the Founding Fathers. *"And you will know the truth [regarding salvation], and the truth will set you free [from the penalty of sin]."* John 8:32
3. Believe that God created certain people groups according to the color of skin, ethnicity, or culture superior/inferior to other people groups.	Know that God created mankind in His image and makes no distinction between race or ethnicity. *"For God shows no partiality [no arbitrary favoritism;* **with Him one person is not more important than another]."** Rom 2:11 [26] *"So in Christ Jesus you are all children of God through faith,* [27] *for all of you who were baptized into Christ have clothed yourselves with Christ.* [28] **There is neither Jew**

	nor Gentile, neither slave nor free, nor is there male and female, for you are all one in Christ Jesus." Gal 3:26-28
4. Believe passing laws and imposing their beliefs against abortion and same-sex marriage, etc. will change people's behavior.	Know that God is both pro-choice and pro-life. Behavior changes in response to choosing to believe in and follow Jesus. *"This day I call the heavens and the earth as witnesses against you that I have **set before you life and death, blessings and curses. Now choose life,** so that you and your children may live."* Deut. 30:19
5. Motivated by the same self-righteous religious spirit that motivated the scribes and Pharisees' when they criticized Jesus for not strictly following the Mosaic law.	Understand that the enforcement of Mosaic law is not the way to reach "sinners". *[8] **For it is by grace [God's remarkable compassion and favor drawing you to Christ] that you have been saved [actually delivered from judgment and given eternal life]** through faith. And this [salvation] **is not of yourselves [not through your own effort], but it is the [undeserved, gracious] gift of** God; [9] not as a result of [your] works [nor your*

	attempts to keep the Law], so that no one will [be able to] boast or take credit in any way [for his salvation]. Eph. 2:8-9
6. Place respecting and pledging allegiance to the American flag of more importance than treating fellow American citizens with honor, respect, and dignity. Vigilant in protecting the unborn yet refuse to protect and provide for the welfare of millions of children born into poverty who lack adequate health care, receive inferior education, and are most vulnerable to being kidnapped into slavery and sex trafficking.	Understand the importance of honoring God in the way they treat others. *35 "For I was hungry and you gave me something to eat, I was thirsty and you gave me something to drink, I was a stranger and you invited me in, 36 I needed clothes and you clothed me, I was sick and you looked after me, I was in prison and you came to visit me.' 37 "Then the righteous will answer him, 'Lord, when did we see you hungry and feed you, or thirsty and give you something to drink? 38 When did we see you a stranger and invite you in, or needing clothes and clothe you? 39 When did we see you sick or in prison and go to visit you?' 40 "The King will reply, **'Truly I tell you, whatever you did for one of the least of these brothers and sisters of mine, you did for me."*** Matt 25:35-40
7. Lack of compassion in their treatment of others, which is demonstrated in	Are motivated by the love of Jesus in their treatment of others.

the many laws that are in place to restrict and disenfranchise non-white US citizens based upon a systemic bias against US citizens of color.	*"By this everyone will know that you are My disciples if **you have love and unselfish concern for one another**."* John 15:13 *"He has told you, O man, what is good; And what does the* LORD *require of you Except to **be just, and to love [and to diligently practice] kindness (compassion)**, And to walk humbly with your God [setting aside any overblown sense of importance or self-righteousness]?* Micah 6:8
8. Equate "conservatism" with Christianity. "Conservative" Christians tend to oppose any legislation that provides support for citizens that are facing health or financial setbacks. Agencies such as the Social Security Administration and the Department of Human Welfare are primarily focused on disqualifying applicants from the services these agencies were established to serve.	Understand the importance to God that we must provide for orphans and widows and outcasts. *"Religion that God our Father accepts as pure and faultless is this: **to look after orphans and widows** in their distress and to keep oneself from being polluted by the world."* James 1:27
9. Believe liberals are anti-Christian.	Understand that in scripture the term liberal means generous and

	noble. To be generous is to be godly. "The **generous man [is a source of blessing and] shall be prosperous and enriched**, And he who waters will himself be watered [reaping the generosity he has sown]." Prov 11:25 "The one who blesses others is abundantly blessed; those who help others are helped. Prov 11:25 But **the noble, openhearted, and liberal man devises noble things; and he stands for what is noble, openhearted, and generous.**" Is 32:8
10. Do not believe in fair and just treatment for every American which is demonstrated in their unwillingness to acknowledge the blatant injustice of the American judicial system towards Americans of color.	Know the importance of advocating for justice for all. Abolitionists were Christians (Quakers) who advocated for and insisted on the abolishment of slavery. The civil rights movement was led by Christian men and women. "For I know how many are your offenses and how great your sins. **There are those who oppress the innocent and take bribes and deprive the poor of**

	justice in the courts." Amos 5:12 *"But let justice roll on like a river, righteousness like a never-failing stream!"* Amos 5:24 **⁸⁻⁹ "Speak up for the people who have no voice, for the rights of all the down-and-outers. Speak out for justice! Stand up for the poor and destitute!"** Prov 31:8-9
11. Are opposed to immigrants, particularly from non-European nations. Support the government in separating immigrant children from their parents.	Understand the importance of defending immigrants. ***"Cursed is he who distorts (perverts) the justice due to a stranger, an orphan, and a widow.'** And all the people shall say, 'Amen.'"* Deut. 27:19 **"He executes justice for the orphan and the widow and shows His love for the stranger (resident alien, foreigner) by giving him food and clothing.**" Deut. 10:18
12. Believe their Constitutional right to carry guns to defend themselves and their property takes priority over living by the Word of God. Their faith is in the Constitution and "law and order".	Understand that executing their Constitutional rights should never override their responsibility to love their neighbor and that Jesus does not condone or approve of violent actions to defend themselves

> against the violent actions of others.
> [51] *"With that, one of Jesus' companions reached for his sword, drew it out, and struck the servant of the high priest, cutting off his ear.* [52] *'**Put your sword back in its place,' Jesus said to him, 'for all who draw the sword will die by the sword.**"* Matt 26:51-52
> [3] *"For though we live in the world, we do not wage war as the world does.* [4] ***The weapons we fight with are not the weapons of the world.*** *On the contrary, they have divine power to demolish strongholds."* 2 Cor 10:3-4

By now you should realize this message is to expose those who embrace American Christianity. I am convinced that hatred towards Americans of African ancestry is systematically embedded in Americanism, and it is the hallmark of American Christianity. What is Americanism? Merriam-Webster defines it as:

- attachment or allegiance to the traditions, interests, or ideals of the U.S.
- a custom or trait peculiar to America
- the political principles and practices essential to American culture

Americanism is entrenched in an ethnocentric attitude and is the god of American Christianity. As I learned from

Founding Father Benjamin Franklin, the original intent of the founding of the United States of America was to use the blood, sweat, and tears of my African ancestors to establish economic and political power and world domination for the benefit of white Europeans and at the same time exclude Blacks from the benefits of their labor. Even though the Emancipation Proclamation was effective as of January 1, 1863, the systemic bondage of African Americans continues to this very day, mainly due to the steadfast dedication of American Christianity to the gospel of Americanism.

Who are the followers of American Christianity? You know who you are. You are the ones who faithfully assembled Sunday, May 24, 2020, to worship and praise God, and then on Tuesday, May 26 watched the lynching of George Floyd, then said and did absolutely nothing to stop this atrocity. You are the preachers who faithfully proclaim the "word of faith" and push the prosperity message that promises wealth to congregants who plant their seeds to reap a harvest, but you remain silent - not speaking up for justice for African Americans. You are the ones who love to quote Dr. Martin Luther King's stance against violence, yet you fail to speak out against the violence inflicted upon Ahmaud Arbery and Breonna Taylor. And when you do speak, it is nothing more than platitudes – banal, trite, stale remarks. I recall hearing Dr. King many times quote Amos 5:24, "**But let justice roll on like a river, righteousness like a never-failing stream!**". Yet over 50 years after Dr. King's violent murder there still is no justice for African Americans.

American Christians, do you know Jesus? Better yet, does Jesus know you? One of the most sobering scriptures in the entire Bible is Mathew 7:21-23:

> [21]Not everyone who says to Me, 'Lord, Lord,' will enter the kingdom of heaven, but only he who does the will of My Father who is in heaven. [22] Many will say to Me

on that day [when I judge them], 'Lord, Lord, have we not prophesied in Your name, and driven out demons in Your name, and done many miracles in Your name?' 23 And then I will declare to them publicly, 'I never knew you; DEPART FROM ME [you are banished from My presence], YOU WHO ACT WICKEDLY [disregarding My commands].'

What a shock to discover after all the sermons you preached, miracles you performed, and demons you drove out in the Name of Jesus you stand before Him in judgment and He tells you, "I never knew you, go to hell".

We are admonished in the first epistle of John 3:18, "Dear children, let us not love with words or speech but with actions and in truth." I invite every Christian in America who has an authentic relationship with Jesus Christ to take action to wipe out and annihilate all vestiges of hatred (racism) by renouncing Americanism. American Christians are responsible for the election of Donald Trump and consequently, he has been used by Satan to unleash the spirit of hatred that rages out of control throughout the nation today.

God's Word declares in 1 John 4:20 that "If anyone says, 'I love God,' and hates (works against) his [Christian] brother **he is a liar**; for the **one who does not love his brother whom he has seen, cannot love God whom he has not seen**." Authentic Christians who truly love God, let us "**Cry aloud, do not hold back; Lift up your voice like a trumpet**" by confronting elected leaders on every level that justice **MUST** prevail for every American, especially African Americans.

Every white preacher standing behind the sacred pulpit this Sunday should instruct his or her congregation on how they must take an active role in protesting against any incidents of injustice against African Americans in their communities.

AMEN!

2 Open Letter to Christian Churches in America

Introduction
When I woke up Wednesday morning, Nov 9, 2016, and learned that Donald Trump had won the election for president of the United States of America I was in shock! How could such a despicable and morally corrupt individual be elected to the most powerful leadership role on planet earth? And then to find out that 80% of his supporters were identified as Evangelical Christians caused me to ask, "why would any follower of Jesus Christ vote for Mr. Trump?"

I must confess that I was never a fan of Mr. Trump even before he decided to run for president. I found his popularity in the media based on his extravagant wealth and extra-marital affairs a complete turn-off. I never understood why so many people wanted to participate in his reality shows: The Apprentice or The Celebrity Apprentice. When he finally declared his candidacy for president, the media gave him almost 100% of their focus, to the exclusion of the many other candidates! Every other candidate deserved the media's acknowledgment, but unfortunately, there was such a frenzy to react to Mr. Trump's senseless tweets and opinions that there was very little coverage of the other candidates. Yes, the media did cover the Democratic candidate, Hillary Clinton, but her coverage seemed to always be in the shadow of Mr. Trump's shenanigans.

Response of Pro-Trump Christians
I still find the response by many American Christians to Donald Trump's election in 2016 and his loss in 2020 problematic. There were several high-profile preachers, pastors of mega-churches, and televangelists with millions of followers who took delight in declaring their support for Mr. Trump. There is one particular woman preacher who received a lot of media attention for being Trump's "spiritual advisor". In the past, I have attended conventions and watched TV with many of these preachers. But I have been turned off from

following their ministries because they supported Mr. Trump.

With all her proclamations that God had chosen Donald Trump to be president, I wondered if his spiritual advisor or any of the other evangelical preachers in Mr. Trump's inner circle had ever taken the time to introduce Mr. Trump to Jesus. Isn't that the evangelical thing to do? Instead, I watched on TV and on various media platforms these preachers gathered around Mr. Trump acting like clowns as they lay their hands on him and prayed over him. Certainly, these mighty men and women of God have read Matthew Chapter 6, which in the Message translation says:

> [5] And when you come before God, don't turn that into a theatrical production either. All these people making a regular show out of their prayers, hoping for fifteen minutes of fame! Do you think God sits in a box seat? [7-8] The world is full of so-called prayer warriors who are prayer-ignorant. They're full of formulas and programs and advice, peddling techniques for getting what you want from God. Don't fall for that nonsense. This is your Father you are dealing with, and he knows better than you what you need.

Instead of sharing the love of Jesus with Mr. Trump, they ingratiated themselves with him to gain his support for their agenda, which was that he opposes passing any laws or policies that threaten their "Christian values" or "religious rights and freedom". Is this what Jesus instructed His followers to do? I have searched the Gospels through and through and have yet to find Jesus telling His disciples that making disciples involves making a nation or government establish laws and policies to protect the rights and freedoms of the followers of Jesus.

Response of Anti-Trump Christians
Then there are the American Christians that were enraged by Mr. Trump's election. I must confess that I was one of them. How in the world could God endorse the election of such a

despicable and morally corrupt individual as Donald Trump? I have overheard many heated discussions and arguments among Christians expressing their disdain for the man. When a Christian singer declared she would pray for Mr. Trump, she was criticized bitterly for even suggesting that Christians should pray for Mr. Trump. Just speaking Trump's name triggers many Christians into angry tirades about what a horrible person he is.

Response of American Christians

So, what do we have? One group of Christians says, "God is for Mr. Trump", and the other group of Christians says, "Trump is of the devil". But both groups ignore the obvious fact that Donald Trump has never met Jesus! With all his wealth, fame, and popularity, he is perhaps the saddest, loneliest, and most frightened man in America. He is so filled with fear, and the Bible does declare that fear has torment (1 John 4:18). Donald Trump is a tormented man who needs Jesus in his life. Sadly, this is the plight of too many Americans who identify as Christians.

When the Holy Spirit helped me recognize this I, like the aforementioned Christian singer, began to pray for Mr. Trump and all the many tormented Americans consumed by hate. After all, didn't Jesus give us specific instructions on what we should do in response to those who hate us? Even though I do not support the politics of Donald Trump, Matthew 5:44 tells me exactly what I must do, "But I tell you, love your enemies and pray for those who persecute you."

The only remedy for fear and hate is the love of God! And for those Christians who fear being persecuted and losing their religious freedom, have you not read what Jesus said throughout the Gospels?

- "Blessed are those who are persecuted because of righteousness, for theirs is the kingdom of heaven." (Matthew 5:10)

- "Blessed are you when people insult you, persecute you, and falsely say all kinds of evil against you because of me." (Matthew 5:11)

- "Rejoice and be glad, because great is your reward in heaven, for, in the same way, they persecuted the prophets who were before you." (Matthew 5:12)

- "Then you will be handed over to be persecuted and put to death, and you will be hated by all nations because of me." (Matthew 24:9)

Jesus did warn us in John 16:33 "I have told you these things, so that in me you may have peace. In this world, you will have trouble. But take heart! I have overcome the world." Just because we live in America, it does not exempt us from persecution in this world. Freedom for believers in Jesus was purchased by His blood on Calvary over 2000 years ago and not the Declaration of Independence, Bill of Rights, or the US Constitution.

As eloquent as these documents may be, they do not have any power in effectuating true freedom. Jesus made it very clear in John 8:31-32, ^{31} "To the Jews who had believed him, Jesus said, If you hold to my teaching, you are really my disciples. ^{32} Then you will know the truth, and the truth will set you free." Please take notice that Jesus was speaking directly to Jews who had already placed their belief in Him. I know of no government or nation, not even the nation of Israel, that has the power to override the freedom offered to those that follow Jesus!

Apostle Paul is highly regarded for writing the vast majority of letters that became canonized in the New Testament. But before Paul met Jesus, he religiously followed Hebrew law and was a vigilante for the enforcement of Hebrew law. He sincerely believed it was his responsibility to persecute every Jew who did not comply with Jewish laws. With the support of the Jewish leaders, he was given the authority to terrorize any and everyone who broke Hebrew law. Paul even confessed, "For I am the least of the apostles and do not even deserve to be called an apostle, because I persecuted the church of God." (1 Corinthians 15:9)

Not everyone's encounter with Jesus is as dramatic as Paul's on the road to Damascus. But every follower of Jesus can testify for a fact that when they came to know Jesus, their life was transformed. It is so sad that the love, grace, and mercy that God freely extends to absolutely everyone is missing from the messaging and actions of American Christians.

Conclusion
Every Christian should look forward to seeing Jesus face-to-face when transitioning from earth to Glory. Of course, every believer wants to hear God say, "Well done, good and faithful servant!" when they stand before Him in judgment. (Matthew 25:21) However, Matthew 7:21-23 contains what I believe is the most sobering passage in the entire Bible.

> [21] Not everyone who says to me, 'Lord, Lord,' will enter the kingdom of heaven, but only the one who does the will of my Father who is in heaven. [22] Many will say to me on that day, 'Lord, Lord, did we not prophesy in your name and in your name drive out demons and, in your name, perform many miracles?' [23] Then I will tell them plainly, 'I never knew you. Away from me, you evildoers!'

How is it possible that anyone who has prophesied, cast out demons, and performed miracles all in the Name of Jesus could be greeted by God with, "I never knew you, go away from me, you evildoers"? Surely such mighty men and women of God would expect to be welcomed by God with outstretched arms! This scripture should cause every Christian to pause and take inventory of their lives and ask themselves the following questions:

1. Do I practice religion, or do I have a genuine relationship with Father God?

   "See what great love the Father has lavished on us, that we should be called children of God! And that is what we are!" (1 John 3:1)

2. Do I need to ask others to pray for me to get an answer to my prayers, or do I follow the instructions of Jesus by pulling away in private and spending intimate one-on-one time talking and listening to Father God?

   "But when you pray, go into your room, close the door and pray to your Father, who is unseen. Then your Father, who sees what is done in secret, will reward you." (Matthew 6:6)

3. Do I spend time complaining about this dark and evil world, or do I let the light of Jesus radiate from my life bringing the presence of God with me wherever I go? Jesus declared:

   [14-16] "Here's another way to put it: You're here to be light, bringing out the God-colors in the world. God is not a secret to be kept. We're going public with this, as public as a city on a hill. If I make you light-bearers, you don't think I'm going to hide you under a bucket, do you? I'm putting you on a light stand. Now that I've put you there on a hilltop, on a light stand—shine! Keep open house; be generous with your lives. By opening up to others, you'll prompt people to open up with God, this generous Father in heaven." (Matthew 5:14-16)

4. Do I complain about my enemies, or do I love them and pray for them?

   "But I tell you, love your enemies and pray for those who persecute you, [45] that you may be children of your

Father in heaven. He causes his sun to rise on the evil and the good, and sends rain on the righteous and the unrighteous." (Matthew 5:44-45)

5. Do I judge others for their sinful ways, or do I recognize their need to meet Jesus and treat them with the same lovingkindness, grace, and mercy God constantly extends to me?

"Don't pick on people, jump on their failures, criticize their faults—unless, of course, you want the same treatment. That critical spirit has a way of boomeranging. It's easy to see a smudge on your neighbor's face and be oblivious to the ugly sneer on your own. Do you have the nerve to say, 'Let me wash your face for you,' when your own face is distorted by contempt? It's this whole traveling road-show mentality all over again, playing a holier-than-thou part instead of just living your part. Wipe that ugly sneer off your own face, and you might be fit to offer a washcloth to your neighbor." (Matthew 7:1-5)

6. Final Question - What do you want to hear the Lord say when you stand before Him in judgment – will it be, "I never knew you, depart from me", or "Well done, good and faithful servant"? (Matthew 25:21,23)

3 Is American Christianity Antichrist? – Where is the Love?

There is an epidemic in the US that is far more deadly than the Covid-19 pandemic. It is **HATE,** and its dominance in America is an indictment against American Christianity! For centuries Americans have boasted that America is a Christian nation. If in fact, American Christians were true believers and disciples of Jesus Christ, they would be following His instructions, [34] "A new command I give you: Love one another. As I have loved you, so you must love one another. [35] By this everyone will know that you are my disciples if you love one another." (John 13:34-35)

In the wake of the political fighting, social unrest, and non-stop violence happening in America today, I ask the resounding question, where is the love? American Christianity promotes a very perverted version of love. What I have discovered about the American version of Christianity is that it is a religious movement that in no way reflects the teachings of Jesus. How can it claim to love God on the one hand yet on the other hand promote hate? The Bible clearly states, [20] "But if we say we love God and don't love each other, we are liars. We cannot see God. So how can we love God, if we don't love the people we can see? [21] The commandment that God has given us is: "Love God and love each other!" (John 4:20-21)

God's love compels His followers to treat all human beings with compassion, dignity, and respect. No matter what label is used – racism, sexism, homophobia, misogyny, xenophobia – the Word of God equates all these attitudes to **hate**.

For many years I have asked myself these questions:

1. Why do American Christians insist upon pushing the false narrative that America was founded on the Christian values of its Founding Fathers when in fact America's founding is the result of the European

colonizers' terroristic takeover of this land from its original inhabitants?

2. Why do American Christians justify the chattel enslavement of Africans and continue to deny humane treatment to their descendants?

3. Why do American Christians approve and justify police killing unarmed men and women particularly those of color?

4. Why do American Christians insist on creating laws that persecute people who do not conform to their pseudo-Christian norm rather than extending to them the compassionate grace and mercy that God provides for all humans?

5. The Gospels record that Jesus was moved with compassion, which is defined as sympathetic consciousness of others' distress and a desire to alleviate it. If American Christians were true disciples of Jesus where is their compassion? If they knew Jesus they would:

    - Oppose all efforts to restrict the voting rights of all American citizens

    - Protect children from sex predators

    - Support provisions of affordable housing for millions of homeless families

    - Insist upon quality education for all children

- Oppose the separation of immigrant children from their parents

- Support provisions of free health care services for all families

The godly response to hatred is not making more laws. Taking a vigilant stance on "Law and Order" and the right to bear arms will never make our communities safe for their citizens. All acts of violence are hate crimes. Didn't Jesus give His instructions on how His followers are to respond to hate?

> [27] But I say to you who hear [Me and pay attention to My words]: [a]Love [that is, unselfishly seek the best or higher good for] your enemies, [make it a practice to] do good to those who hate you, [28] bless *and* show kindness to those who curse you, pray for those who mistreat you. [29] Whoever [b]strikes you on the cheek, offer him the other one also [simply ignore insignificant insults or losses and do not bother to retaliate—maintain your dignity]. Whoever takes away your coat, do not withhold your shirt from him either. [30] Give to everyone who asks of you. [c]Whoever takes away what is yours, do not demand it back. [31] Treat others the same way you want them to treat you. (Luke 6:27-31)

God proved in the Hebrew Bible that even His laws did not change the behavior of the Israelite people. God only gave the Israelites 10 commandments to obey. They would keep His commandments for a short period then slip back into disobedience time and time again. That is why He sent Jesus to save us from our sinful nature and Jesus sent the Holy Spirit to empower us to obey His word. It is only by the Holy Spirit that we can conduct our lives in a way that honors and pleases Father God.

The National Day of Prayer is observed each year in May. The following was extracted from the National Day of Prayer website:

> The National Day of Prayer is an annual observance held on the first Thursday of May, inviting people of all faiths to pray for the nation. It was created in 1952 by a joint resolution of the United States Congress and signed into law by President Harry S. Truman. Our Task Force is a privately funded organization whose purpose is to encourage participation on the National Day of Prayer. It exists to communicate with every individual the need for personal repentance and prayer, to create appropriate materials, and to mobilize the Christian community to intercede for America's leaders and its families. **The Task Force represents a Judeo-Christian expression of the national observance, based on our understanding that this country was birthed in prayer and reverence for the God of the Bible.**

Although this description sounds very impressive, the final statement is absolutely false. This country was **NOT** birthed in prayer and reverence for the God of the Bible!

My pastor in the '90s was a staunch supporter of the anti-abortion/pro-life movement. During that period a tragic event occurred in which an anti-abortion vigilante shot and killed Dr. David Gunn who performed abortions in Pensacola, Florida. Much to my dismay, my pastor declared from the pulpit that the doctor should have been killed.

My observation is that American Christians are the haters. This group has been labeled as Evangelicals and White Conservatives. However, anti-abortion/pro-life beliefs also exist among many Christians of color as well. American Christianity whitewashes the teachings of Jesus and is the instigator of racism in America. I believe that American Christianity is a political movement that uses religion to impose its norms on those they consider to be "other" and beneath themselves.

It appears that American Christianity is infected by the antichrist spirit. How did this twisted version of Christianity come about? How did Christianity in America become such a travesty? Seeking answers to my questions I consulted with Dr. Curtis Dodson, anointed and highly respected eschatologist and Chancellor of The Word Wise Institute of Eschatology, who provided the following definition/description of the spirit of the antichrist: *"Any actions, words, deeds, or behaviors that distort, marginalize, minimize, demean, cloud, disrupt, dishonor, demote, bring down, or misrepresent the image of Christ, His Church, or His message of love to the world."*

This is exactly what was manifested in American Christianity from its very beginning. It is clear to me that American Christianity was founded by the spirit of the antichrist operating in the hearts of the Founding Fathers. The freedom and independence they fought for were exclusively for white male property owners. Their concept of freedom was not extended to women or people of color, especially the enslaved Africans.

The Gospel of Jesus Christ has been hijacked by the spirit of the antichrist in the messaging of many American Christian preachers. Instead of spreading the good news of salvation offered by Jesus, unfortunately, some American Christians have been seduced into religion. It appears that far too many American Christians are guilty of promoting religion rather than introducing non-believers to an authentic relationship with Christ Jesus.

Over the years, many Christian leaders have spent an extraordinary amount of effort promoting issues such as insisting that prayer be allowed in public schools and opposing the legalization of same-sex marriage. First of all, man cannot control who and how we can talk with God. Public prayer is not required of any followers of Jesus. Jesus clearly stated that prayer is not for public display. "But when you pray, go into your most private room, close the door and pray to your Father who is in secret, and your Father who sees [what is done] in secret will reward you." (Matthew 6:6)

Through the Gospels, it is recorded that Jesus would pull away from the disciples and the crowds to spend time in private conversations (prayer) with God. Shouldn't we follow His example? By the way, marriage is God's idea, not man's. A man may try to create and enforce laws concerning marriage, but only God can unite a man and woman in holy matrimony. Man-made unions are simply man-made unions. God is Creator. Satan has no creative power whatsoever and only tries to steal, kill and destroy God's creative work. Man can't create laws that can override God's commandments. Authentic Christians do not need to waste their energy passing laws to make nonbelievers stop sinning.

Even though it is God's perfect will that everyone chooses to accept Jesus as Lord and Savior (2 Peter 3:9), He does not override anyone's will with His will! Yes, John 3:16 does declare that God loves everyone so much that He sacrificed His only begotten son so that whoever believes in Him will not perish but have eternal life. But why do so many Christians fail to acknowledge the very next verse? "For God did not send the Son into the world to judge *and* condemn the world [that is, to initiate the final judgment of the world], but that the world might be saved through Him." (John 3:17)

As much as God desires us to choose Him, He refuses to force His will upon us. Instead, He draws us to Himself through His love, grace, and mercy. "For long ago the Lord had said to Israel: I have loved you, O my people, with an everlasting love; with loving-kindness, I have drawn you to me." (Jeremiah 31:3) Whether addressing the Jews of the Old Testament or Gentiles in the New Testament, it is God's modus operandi to woo us with His lovingkindness. How dare American Christians demand anyone to live their lives according to their religious demands!

American Christians so often totally misrepresent the image of Christ when spewing words of judgment and hate that are absolutely antichrist! Authentic Christians compassionately share Jesus' message of love, redemption, and salvation. True followers of Jesus faithfully obey His teachings by introducing non-believers to Jesus knowing that it only takes an encounter with Jesus to transform a life from its sinful nature into a redeemed believer and follower of Jesus Christ. It is so important that we keep in mind that God's purpose for sending Jesus was all about redemption and restoration. Jesus' birth, death, and resurrection were to redeem our lives from our sinful nature so that our relationship with God can be restored to the relationship that Adam and Eve had when they were in the Garden of Eden. As declared in John 3:17 "God didn't go to all the trouble of sending his Son merely to point an accusing finger, telling the world how bad it was. He came to help, to put the world right again."

Instead of sharing the love of Jesus, American Christians are in a religious frenzy that creates and supports laws and policies designed to coerce non-believers to conduct their lives according to their "Christian values" or "religious rights and freedom". During this Covid-19 pandemic, I am hard-pressed to recognize the love of God demonstrated in the lives of many American Christians. Those who are resistant to taking the Covid-19 vaccine or wearing a face mask because they feel their rights are being taken away evidently have no love for God or their neighbors. We are in the midst of a public health crisis and God has provided scientists with a vaccine that can save lives. If American Christians truly love God and their neighbors, they would choose to comply with the provisions God has provided us to overcome this virus. It is obvious to me that the fear and selfishness that have gripped the hearts and minds of millions of Americans are a manifestation of the spirit of the antichrist. I must repeat Dr.

Dodson's definition of the antichrist spirit: *"*Any actions, words, deeds, or behaviors that distort, marginalize, minimize, demean, cloud, disrupt, dishonor, demote, bring down, or misrepresent the image of Christ, His Church or His message of love to the world.*"*

If America is indeed a Christian nation, where is the love?

4 Is American Christianity Antichrist? – The Most Divided Hour in America

How is it that American preachers, on one hand, can preach the gospel of Jesus Christ which is the Truth that sets us free, and on the other hand preach that America was birthed in prayer and in reverence for the God of the Bible which is not true?

Black Americans have been writing and speaking out against the racism of white American Christians for decades. Frederick Douglass, preeminent abolitionist, statesman, writer and orator, and former slave was invited to speak in Rochester, New York, on July 5, 1852, on the 76th anniversary of the signing of the Declaration of Independence. His scathing speech was entitled "What to the Slave is the Fourth of July?" I found the following excerpts from his speech absolutely brilliant!

> This Fourth of July is *yours,* not *mine.* You may rejoice, I must mourn, do you mean, citizens, to mock me, by asking me to speak today?
>
> What, to the American slave, is your 4th of July? I answer; a day that reveals to him, more than all other days in the year, the gross injustice and cruelty to which he is the constant victim.
>
> To him, your celebration is a sham; your boasted liberty, an unholy license; your national greatness, swelling vanity; your sound of rejoicing are empty and heartless; your denunciation of tyrants brass fronted impudence; your shout of liberty and equality, hollow mockery; your prayers and hymns, your sermons and thanksgivings, with all your religious parade and solemnity, are to him, mere bombast, fraud, deception, impiety, and hypocrisy — a thin veil to cover up crimes which would disgrace a nation of savages.

Amen, Mr. Douglass, Amen!

As I continued my research to validate my hypothesis, I was amazed at the number of books, articles, and videos by white Americans that address the phenomena of White American Christianity. As previously stated, black Americans have been speaking and writing and protesting against racism for years, but for me to learn that there are many white Americans who recognize that racism was and continues to be promoted by white Christian Americans is a game changer!

I was first introduced to the term White Christian America by reading books authored by Dr. Robert P Jones. His book, *The End of White Christian America* was mind-boggling! He used the term White Christian America to refer to the cultural domain populated exclusively by white mainline and evangelical Protestants (p. 38). He even admitted that "white Protestantism as a whole is arguably the most powerful cultural force in the history of our country." His extensive research revealed that while the theology and culture of White Christian America have dominated life in America from its very beginning, he also acknowledged his research reveals that its power is on the verge of dying due to powerful demographic changes within America. Dr. Jones revealed that due to the fact the percentage of Americans of color is increasing and the percentage of white Americans is decreasing this is most unsettling for White Christian America. (p. 40)

Like many Americans, both black and white, I celebrated the election of our first president of African descent in 2008. However, I was quite dismayed by the pushback he received from white members of Congress once he was in office. Dr. Jones' observation of the impact of the election of Barak Obama is absolutely on point! He stated, "The intensely negative reactions to his presidency among some whites – in particular, a series of challenges to the authenticity of his citizenship and his faith – were certainly fueled by the fact that he does not come from the world of White Christian America". (p. 41)

I lived in a suburb of DC during President Obama's tenure and the negativity in the DC metropolitan area was tense and visceral. Throughout his eight years as president, I avoided having conversations, both at church and work, with "friends" who did not like President Obama. Never in a million years could I have imagined that a man like Donald Trump would be elected president of the United States of America. How did we go from electing a person of such dignity, grace, and service-mindedness as Barak Obama to electing a person so crass, self-absorbed, narcissistic, and morally corrupt as Donald Trump? I cannot help but suspect that Trump's election was the result of hate-inspired backlash from white Americans, both Christian and non-Christian.

In his chapter entitled "Race: Desegregating White Christian America" Jones' research exposed some profound differences between white Americans' perception of reality and the reality perception of Americans of African descent. Jones revealed that there is a definite racial perception gap in the treatment of blacks and other minorities in the criminal justice system. Public opinion data gathered from various resources showed that:

1. After the April 2015 protests and riots in Baltimore, a Public Religion Research Institute (PRRI) survey asked Americans whether they thought "the recent killings of African American men by police in Ferguson, Missouri, New York City, and Baltimore" were "isolated incidents" or "part of a broader pattern of how police treat African Americans." Nearly three-quarters (74%) of black Americans said that these incidents were part of a broader pattern. Among white Americans by contrast, only 43% of white Americans saw the men's death as part of a larger pattern; roughly the same number (45%) saw these events as isolated incidents. (p.153-154)

2. The racial perception gap between white evangelical Protestants and African Americans is a yawning 45 percentage points. Fewer than three in ten (29%) white evangelical Protestants see the recent killings of black men by police as part of a broader pattern, while 57% see them as isolated incidents. (p.154-155)

I can't help but join Dr. Jones in asking the question: Why can't White Christian America understand how African Americans feel about the black men who have died at the hands of white police officers? (p.155)

I was amazed to see the number of whites that took to the streets all across America and around the world to protest against the May 2020 murder of George Floyd, an American of African descent. The video of Mr. Floyd being callously choked to death by a white police officer provoked an outcry from people on every continent and every race, culture, nationality, and ethnicity. There were even protests by inhabitants of mid-west American towns that had no black residents! It is obvious to me that a human being does not have to be Christian to recognize inhumane treatment by one human to another human. After decades of police officers being exonerated for killing innocent African Americans, it seemed like a miracle when the jury found the police officer who killed Mr. Floyd guilty as charged!

From a 2013 Public Religion Research Institute (PRRI) survey Jones learned that staggering levels of segregation exist within Americans' social networks. The survey found that, on average, the core social networks of white Americans are a remarkable 91% white and only one percent black. Moreover, three-quarters of white Americans have completely white core social networks. (p.159) Another staggering revelation of this survey was that among white evangelicals and mainline Protestants, these levels of homogeneity are even higher. Fully eight in ten white evangelical Protestants and 85% of white mainline Protestants have entirely white core social!

networks. (p.159) How astounding that white Christian Americans tend to segregate themselves from blacks more so than white non-Christian Americans

As a result of the Civil Rights Movement of the '60s, progress has been made in the integration of workspaces and educational institutions. However, one segment of American society that continues to be gripped by hate (racism, sexism, homophobia, xenophobia, etc.) is its religious organizations – specifically the Christian Church. In an interview on "Meet The Press" on April 17, 1960, the late Rev. Dr. Martin Luther King Jr. stated, "11 AM Sunday morning is the most segregated hour in Christian America".

Sadly, his statement is still true over 60 years later. Dr. Jones echoed the words of Dr. King in stating "…however deeply the principles of racial equality may be enshrined in theology and liturgy, they have had little impact on the actual racial composition of Christian congregations, past or present." (p.163-164) Dr. Jones referenced the following observations made by Protestant theologian H. Richard Niebuhr in his book *The Social Sources of Denominationalism*.

> …denominational divisions within the American Protestant churches – which fell along racial, ethnic, and class lines – were a glaring ethical failure.
> The division of the churches closely follows the division of men into the castes of national, racial, and economic groups. It draws the color line in the church of God.
>
> Niebuhr noted that nearly 90% of all African American Christians in the 1920s were members of churches affiliated exclusively with black denominations, and nearly all of the remainder were restricted to special conferences within white denominations. (p.164)

I appreciate Niebuhr's critique of denominations. I have always wondered why the church is divided into denominations. Early in my Christian journey, I learned that

Jesus Christ is the "Head" of the church and the "Body of Christ" is a metaphor for the church. If Jesus and the church together are one entity, how is it possible for one head to be attached to so many different bodies? The image of that would look like a monster in a horror movie! Does American Christianity practice authentic Christianity?

In the Living Bible Translation of Romans 15:5-7 Apostle Paul instructs the church:

> 5 "May God who gives patience, steadiness, and encouragement help you to **live in complete harmony with each other—each with the attitude of Christ toward the other**. 6 And then all of us can praise the Lord together with one voice, giving glory to God, the Father of our Lord Jesus Christ. 7 So **warmly welcome each other into the church, just as Christ has warmly welcomed you**; then God will be glorified."

Where is harmony both within and between denominations? The concept of denomination focuses on differences! How does this give glory to God? Can we genuinely praise the Lord and give glory to God while at the same time not welcoming others into the church? These scriptures clearly reveal that the practice of denominationalism is of the antichrist spirit!

I totally agree with Dr. Jones' observation that the principles of Christianity have had little impact on the actual racial composition of American Christian congregations, past or present. Although I attended schools with whites, attending church was an exclusively black experience for my family. The church I grew up attending was the Church o God in Christ (COGIC), a predominantly black Pentecostal denomination. Church for me and my siblings was always fun and exciting because of the awesome singing and joyful dancing. But being Pentecostal during my childhood years was something I avoided advertising to our friends in the neighborhood. At that time Pentecostals were looked down upon and even ostracized by those who attended the more traditional mainline denominations such as Baptist or Methodist.

I was in my thirties before attending a church service attended by blacks and whites. I was a seminary student at Howard University School of Divinity (HUSD) when I learned of the origins of American black church denominations. The enslaved African Americans were allowed to worship with whites but were restricted from sitting with white congregants. Black churches were created and organized by people of African descent as a response to being officially discriminated against by white congregations. The African Methodist Episcopal (AME) Church is the first Protestant denomination to be founded by black people in America.

Black churches created communities and worship practices that were culturally distinct from other churches, including forms of Christian worship that derived from African spiritual traditions, such as call and response. These churches also became the centers of communities, serving as school sites, taking up social welfare functions such as providing for the indigent and going on to establish orphanages and prison ministries. As a result, black churches were particularly important during the Civil Rights Movement. Black churches were where participants of civil rights marches met to plan, train, strategize and pray.

Although most black churches formed as a result of the racist attitude and practices in white churches, I was intrigued to learn that this was not the case in the founding of the COGIC by Charles Harrison Mason. In his book, *Bishop C. H. Mason and the Roots of the Church of God in Christ*, Bishop Ithiel C. Clemmons revealed how the denomination was originally founded by Baptist preachers Charles Harrison Mason and Charles Price Jones in 1897 when they collaborated in their participation in the holiness movement and were eventually excommunicated from the Baptist convention. In 1907 Mason traveled to Los Angeles where he performed a critical task at the Azusa Revival. It appears that he was the only early convert whose church was legally incorporated and could ordain clergy whose status would be recognized by civil authorities as indicated in the following:

> Scores of white ministers sought ordination at the hands of Mason. Large numbers of white ministers, therefore, were to obtain ministerial credentials carrying the name of the Church of God in Christ. Mason and the Church of God in Christ provided ecclesiastical guidance and development for scores of churches among whites across the United States as a result of Pentecostal and holiness revivalism. Moreover, where local congregations of the Church of God in Christ were founded, black and white Saints worked, worshiped, and evangelized together in an interracial, egalitarian fellowship modeled after the interracial fellowship at Azusa Street. (p. 27)

Most American Christians celebrate the Azusa Revival as the event where Christians received baptism in the Holy Spirit accompanied by the phenomenon of speaking in tongues. But I believe that the true evidence of the Holy Spirit was manifested by the fact that:

> ...local congregations of the Church of God in Christ were founded, black and white Saints worked, worshiped, and evangelized together in an interracial, egalitarian fellowship modeled after the interracial fellowship at Azusa Street. This occurred throughout the South including Mississippi, Tennessee, Arkansas, Florida, Louisiana, Alabama, and Georgia during the most racially tense time in the United States. (p. 27)

Every Pentecostal denomination in America, black and white, can trace its roots to the Los Angeles Azusa Revival and COGIC. Although today COGIC is predominantly black, it was not so in its beginnings at Azusa. Sadly, whites pulled away from COGIC to form The Assemblies of God USA, officially the General Council of the Assemblies of God, a Pentecostal Christian denomination in the United States, founded in 1914, because they did not want to continue to be under black leadership. How ironic that most black churches were formed because of whites' racist treatment of the black congregants whereas Charles Mason warmly received and ordained people of all races into the Church of God in Christ, but whites chose to separate themselves from black congregants to form their white-only church organizations.

How amazing that after experiencing the outpouring of the Holy Spirit at Azusa Street, the interracial fellowship was initiated for the first time in American history. Why would the whites break away? Was it because the spirit of white supremacy was more powerful than the Holy Spirit?

From my childhood, I have heard it preached that speaking in tongues is evidence of Holy Spirit baptism. But I discern that the true evidence of Holy Spirit baptism is that it empowers followers of Jesus Christ to worship and serve God as one body without being divided by race, ethnicity, social status, man-made doctrines, or denomination. We are informed in Galatians 5:

> [22] But the fruit of the Spirit [the result of His presence within us] is love [unselfish concern for others], joy, [inner] peace, patience [not the ability to wait, but how we act while waiting], kindness, goodness, faithfulness, [23] gentleness, self-control. Against such things, there is no law.

The evidence of the Holy Spirit is manifested in the fruit of unselfish concern for others, joy, peace, patience, kindness, faithfulness, gentleness, and self-control. Speaking in tongues is meaningless if the transformative power of the Holy Spirit that united people of all racial and ethnic origins at the Azusa Revival is ignored!

The bottom line is this - After the excitement of being baptized by the Holy Spirit and speaking in tongues wore off, white

American Christians returned to their hateful antichrist behavior.

5 Is American Christianity Antichrist? – White Supremacy Continues to Reign

As a disciple of Jesus, I have come to realize that there is a huge disparity between how many white Christians interpret and apply the teachings of Jesus and how many black Christians interpret and apply the teachings of Jesus. It is also common knowledge that there is an ongoing difference between the treatment of white Americans and the treatment of non-white Americans. This was proven by Jane Elliott, an internationally known teacher, lecturer, and diversity trainer when she asked a group of white adult students to raise their hands if anyone would not mind being treated the same way blacks are treated, and none of the students raised their hands.

For some time, I have suspected that the disparities are rooted in white Christians' interpretation of scripture. White Christians take great pride in declaring America was founded as a Christian nation and based upon this false narrative they believe this gives them the right (privilege) to establish laws, policies, and systems that support their "god-ordained" agenda. However, when I read another book authored by Dr. Robert P Jones, *White Too Long: The Legacy of White Supremacy in American Christianity,* the very first statement in his book verified that my suspicion is absolutely correct! Dr. Jones candidly revealed that his family history was entrenched in perpetuating the American legacy of racism in his opening statement: "The Christian denomination in which I grew up was founded on the proposition that chattel slavery could flourish alongside the gospel of Jesus Christ. Its founders believed this arrangement was not just possible but also divinely mandated." *(p.1)*

I have nothing but the utmost respect for Dr. Jones and greatly appreciate his candor in the revelation of his insightful research and writing. However, it mystifies me how his ancestors could profess to be followers of Jesus while holding to the belief that God sanctioned their enslavement of my ancestors. Throughout his book, Jones made profound revelations that shook me to my core, such as the following:

> ...this book – the story of just how intractably white supremacy has become embedded in the DNA of American Christianity – is also personal. The 1815 family Bible on the top shelf of the bookcase in our home library gives witness to ancestors from middle Georgia who were Baptist preachers, slave owners, and Confederate soldiers. (p.3)
>
> American Christianity's theological core has been thoroughly structured by an interest in protecting white supremacy. (p.6)
>
> ...white churches produced such a strong sense of safety and security for those of us who were inside the institution is why it is so hard for white Christians to see the harm it did to those who were outside it, particularly African Americans, and the other kinds of damage it did to us, numbing our own moral sensibilities and limiting our religious development. (p. 75)
>
> The mythology – really the lie – that white Christians tell ourselves, on the few occasions we face our history, is that Christianity has been a force for unambiguous good in the world. No matter what evil Christians commit or what violence Christian institutions justify, an idealized conception of Christianity remains unscathed. This conviction is so deep that evidence to the contrary is simply dismissed. (p. 76)

I just do not understand how it is possible for anyone who has placed their faith in Jesus and received His gift of salvation can form such self-righteous and hateful beliefs. What Bible were they reading? Then I discovered they even dared to create a version of the Bible to justify slavery! The slave Bible was constructed specifically to help white Christian missionaries emphasize passages demanding obedience to masters and to exclude passages suggesting equality or liberation. (p. 77)

Obviously, they failed to read Deuteronomy 4:2 which states, **"You shall not add to the word which I am commanding you, nor take away from it,** so that you may keep the commandments of the LORD your God which I am commanding you."

How arrogant of white Christians to manipulate Holy Scripture to oppress my ancestors. Could such thinking be what Apostle Paul warned of in 1 Timothy 4:1-2? "But the [Holy] Spirit explicitly *and* unmistakably declares that in later times some will turn away from the faith, paying attention instead to deceitful *and* seductive spirits and doctrines of demons, ² **[misled] by the hypocrisy of liars whose consciences are seared as with a branding iron [leaving them incapable of ethical functioning]?"** Like Paul, I believe such beliefs were and still are delusional, irrational, and antichrist!

Jones also revealed that many white Christian abolitionists simultaneously opposed the specific practice of chattel slavery while maintaining core white supremacist attitudes. (p. 91) This shocked me because all these years I believed that white abolitionists fought for the abolishment of slavery because of their Christian faith. I cannot comprehend how anyone can maintain a white supremacist attitude and a love for Jesus at the same time. There is absolutely no way that hate and love can coexist in a person's heart. Apostle Paul warned Timothy of those people **"holding to a form of [outward] godliness (religion), although they have denied its power [for their conduct nullifies their claim of faith].** Avoid such people and keep far away from them." (2 Tim. 3:5)

Unfortunately, this describes far too many American Christians. I was shocked again to learn of the response of

Billy Graham, a highly revered evangelist, to Dr. Martin Luther King Jr's 1963 **I Have A Dream** speech in which he envisioned his children playing with white children, Graham replied, *"Only when Christ comes again will little white children of Alabama walk hand in hand with little black children."* (p. 94)

Did Graham not believe that God can change a stony heart of hatred as declared in Ezekiel 19:11, *"And I will give them one heart [a new heart], and put a new spirit within them. I will take from them the heart of stone, and will give them a heart of flesh [that is responsive to My touch]."* (AMP)

If God can change the hate-filled heart of Saul into Apostle Paul and use him as one of the most effective messengers of the Gospel of Jesus Christ, surely God can do the same for anyone today. We don't have to look very far for an example. Governor George Wallace of Alabama, an outspoken 20th-century segregationist is proof of God's ability to change a stony heart when in the 1972 presidential campaign he announced he no longer supported segregation.

I agree with Jones' observation of the evangelical tradition:

> It's nothing short of astonishing that a religious tradition with this relentless emphasis on salvation and one so hyper-attuned to personal sin can simultaneously maintain such blindness to social sins swirling about it, such as slavery and race-based segregation and bigotry. African American observers of Christianity, from Frederick Douglass to Martin Luther King Jr., have been utterly mystified at the paradox. (p. 96)

Yes, I am mystified by the paradox as well! I keep asking myself "Do white American Christians believe the gospel of Jesus Christ?" Or, are they like the Galatians whom Paul addressed in Gal 1:6-9?

> 6 "I am astonished that you are so quickly deserting the

one who called you to live in the grace of Christ and are turning to a different gospel— 7 which is really no gospel at all. Evidently, some people are throwing you into confusion and are trying to pervert the gospel of Christ. 8 But even if we or an angel from heaven should preach a gospel other than the one, we preached to you, let them be under God's curse! 9 As we have already said, so now I say again: If anybody is preaching to you a gospel other than what you accepted, let them be under God's curse!

American Christians pervert the gospel of Christ in both words and deeds and they are definitely under the control of the antichrist spirit. As I continued reading this book, I kept asking myself "Do these people know Jesus from the Bible?" The thinking of white American Christians has to be twisted to embrace the ungodly attitudes and beliefs of white supremacy. Jones must have had similar feelings when he asked the question: "How prevalent are racist and white supremacist attitudes among white Christians today?" (p.155) Jones conducted extensive research surveying the racial attitudes of both Christian and non-Christian white Americans and the analysis of his findings caused him to draw the following conclusions:

> Religiously unaffiliated whites stand closer than white Christians do to their African American Christian brothers and sisters. (p.163)

> If you were recruiting for a white supremacist cause on a Sunday morning, you'd likely have more success hanging out in the parking lot of an average white Christian church – evangelical Protestant, mainline Protestant, or Catholic – than approaching whites sitting out services at the local coffee shop. (p.185)

> Higher levels of racism are associated with higher probabilities of identifying as a white Christian; and conversely, adding Christianity to the average white

person's identity moves him or her toward more, not less, an affinity for white supremacy. White supremacy lives on today not just in explicitly and consciously held attitudes among white Christians; it has become deeply integrated into the DNA of white Christianity itself. (p.187)

I appreciate Jones' transparency in admitting, "As I've moved through the process of writing this book, of retelling my own story, however, I've been astonished at how ubiquitous the claims of white supremacy have been on my life." (p. 221)

Jones assigned the title "Reckoning – Toward Responsibility and Repair" to the last chapter of his book. I believe that his concept of responsibility and repair does align with God's agenda of redemption and restoration expressed in John 3:16 -17. Verse 16 makes it known that God's love for humankind motivated Him to make it possible for humankind to be redeemed from the penalties of their sinfulness, and Verse 17 clearly states that God did not send his Son into the world to condemn it but to save it. God ultimately wants to restore/repair humankind to the relationship He had with Adam in the Garden of Eden before he disobeyed God and opened the door that permitted the entry of sin into the world.

Another compelling observation by Jones states the following:

> We have allowed white supremacy to separate us not just from our black brothers and sisters but also from a true sense of who we are. It is white Christian souls that have been most disfigured by the myth of white supremacy. (p. 232)

Jones unequivocally agrees the crux of the matter is that white supremacy is "the white problem", a declaration made in the sixties by James Baldwin, African American novelist, playwright, essayist, poet, and activist. To Baldwin's declaration, I must add that the "white problem" continues to be the burden of being black in America. From childhood to adulthood, I have felt encumbered to constrain what I say and do to accommodate the comfort of white Americans. It was only when I reached a level of spiritual maturity where I truly know and embrace who I am in Christ Jesus that I am free to conduct my life in a way that honors God, no matter what others may think of me.

Jones came to the following conclusion:

> We white Christians must find the courage to face the fact that the version of Christianity that our ancestors built – 'the faith of our fathers,' as the hymn celebrates it – was a cultural force that, by design, protected and propagated white supremacy. We have inherited this tradition with scant critique, and we have a moral and religious obligation to face the burden of that history and its demand on our present. (p. 234)

Amen, Dr. Jones, Amen!

The United States of America is not the only nation where white supremacy reigns. Christianity and white supremacy have been strange bedfellows well before the colonization of the Americas. The tendency for one group of people to dominate, discriminate, and oppress another group of people based upon some arbitrary differences existed even during the time of Jesus. Just consider Jesus's ride-or-die disciple Peter. Although Peter was selected by Jesus to be part of His inner circle of disciples, he struggled with accepting non-Jews (gentiles) as Christians. Looking back on world history there is no doubt in my mind that the Crusades which were military expeditions undertaken by Christian powers in the 11th, 12th, and 13th centuries to win the Holy Land from the Muslims, were fueled by white supremacy. Colonialism by Europeans starting with the 15th century was the practice of extending and maintaining a nation's political and economic control over another people or area that was also fueled by white supremacy.

God is love (1 John 4:8), which is the hallmark of authentic Christianity. The love of God is expressed through the outpouring of His lovingkindness, mercy, and grace. No one is excluded from God's love (Rom. 5:8) no matter who they are or even how badly they behave. Nowhere in His teachings did Jesus give privilege and power to one people group over another. God's ultimate goal is that all humankind be reconciled with Him (2 Cor. 5:18). White supremacy and racism are antithetical to the teachings of Jesus because such attitudes are rooted in hate. The American version of Christianity promotes hate whereas authentic Christianity promotes love. Americans take great pride in declaring their allegiance to the flag, "I pledge allegiance to the Flag of the United States of America, and to the Republic for which it stands, one Nation under God, indivisible, with liberty and justice for all."

Truth is, "One nation under God" does not exist. As a nation, America only exists for the benefit of white Christian Americans and does not include people categorized as "other" (people of color, females, LGBTQ, immigrants, etc.). There is no true liberty or justice for those categorized as "other". America is divided more today than ever before. I am convinced that the love of God is missing in the messaging and behavior of American Christians solely because many are under the rule of the antichrist spirit. When Christians submit to the spirit of the antichrist, they are unable to worship God in Spirit and Truth or treat their neighbors with the love of God. When Christians love their neighbor, they will insist that liberty and justice be extended to everyone, not just to some. We love to say "God bless America" but until Christians in America bless and honor God their actions will continue to produce strife, discord, hatred, violence, and the antichrist spirit will continue to terrorize America.

When Christians in America bless and honor God in word and deed, God can bless America!

6 Is a Christian Nation a Possibility?

My Introduction to Christian Nationalism

I grew up in a Christian family. My mom and dad immediately introduced me to Jesus as an infant. My father was a minister in the Church of God in Christ (COGIC), a Pentecostal denomination and my mother was an elementary school teacher. As I look back over my life, I now recognize that my father was the source of my introduction to Christian nationalism ideology. In the sixties, I overheard my father adamantly protesting against the movement to take prayer out of school. However, I do not recall my mom ever protesting about prayer not being allowed in schools. I do remember how adamant she was about not letting my siblings and me leave the house for school before she prayed over us. This was the practice that she learned from her mother who prayed for my mother and her siblings before they left for school each day. I also recall my mother saying that she did not know what God other people prayed to but she knew the God she prayed to and did not trust any unknown person praying over her children.

My church experience was primarily in black congregations until I moved from Los Angeles, California to Dallas, Texas. Initially, I attended a COGIC congregation in Dallas. After a few years, God led me to a non-denominational charismatic Word of Faith church, pastored by a man receiving a lot of attention from the church world and secular media. This was my first experience joining a predominantly white congregation. One thing I found uncomfortable was how the pastor's wife would speak so disparagingly of then-President Carter and she was very vocal about her support for electing Ronald Reagan for president. I lived in California under Reagan's regime as governor and was prevented from pursuing a career in social work when he imposed legislation that caused over 1,000 social workers to be laid off or demoted just as I was about to graduate with my degree in social work. I had no intention of voting for him for president. This church presented a continuous stream of preachers from the Who's Who in the Word of Faith movement. Faith and Prosperity were the buzzwords in the charismatic congregations of the 80s.

I watched Trinity Broadcast Network (TBN) faithfully when it first launched in the early 70s. At that time the teaching and preaching were focused on evangelizing the world for Jesus. I even had friends who volunteered to answer the TBN phones from people calling for prayer and to receive the gift of salvation. But in the 80s I began to notice Christian TV becoming politicized. I will never forget watching a black former NFL player when he announced on TBN that he was changing his party preference to Republican because he believed they better supported Christian values and that he intended to support Reagan's bid for president. One high-profile televangelist declared his candidacy for president with the Republican party in 1988. I never understood where people get the idea that being Republican is equivalent to being Christian.

As the messaging from Christian television became more and more politicized, I began to watch it less often and eventually stopped watching TBN in the 90s. I could not agree with what I heard the televangelist "prophets" saying. Perhaps the Holy Spirit was telling me then that something was amiss.

Where did Christians get the idea that Americans can be made Christians through politics and legislation? Have they forgotten the 18th Amendment to the U.S. Constitution—which banned the manufacture, transportation, and sale of intoxicating liquors that went into effect on January 17, 1920, but was repealed with the passage of the Twenty-first Amendment on December 5, 1933? Will American Christians ever come to realize that creating laws against "immoral" behavior is not the method Jesus taught His disciples to share the Gospel of Jesus Christ? It is Jesus who saves, not man-made laws!

What Is Christian Nationalism?

I read an article written by Ed Stetzer, dean, and professor *at* Wheaton College, in which he presented his critique of comments of former Trump national security adviser Michael Flynn made on Nov. 13, 2021, at the "Re-Awaken America Tour" in San Antonio. This meeting was held at a church pastored by a high-profile minister who is known for his insistence that the US must support the nation of Israel to secure God's blessings upon America. Stetzer observed that Flynn followed the pattern of Christian nationalism by taking a biblical passage aimed at Christ's disciples and applying it to the United States. The following statements were made by Flynn - "If we are going to have one nation under God – which we must – we have to have one religion" and "You have to believe this, that God Almighty is, like, involved in this country, because this is it. ...This is the shining city on the hill."

FYI - Flynn pleaded guilty to lying to the FBI and was pardoned by then-President Donald Trump in November 2020. Obviously, Flynn failed to read number nine of the Ten Commandments which states "Thou shall not lie". I agree with Stetzer's critique of Flynn, "By identifying America as God's chosen nation and calling for a religious establishment, Flynn and others offer a gospel mission that is a distorted caricature of the one to which Christians are called". Amen, Dr. Stetzer, Amen!

Knowing and quoting scripture or attending a church service does not make one a Christian. I was flabbergasted when I discovered the following headline "Putin Quotes Jesus To Justify Invasion Of Ukraine" for a March 19, 2022 article by Grayson Quay weekend editor at *TheWeek.com*. Russian President Vladimir Putin identifies as a Russian Orthodox Christian. How is it that a person so full of and tormented by hate can identify himself as a Christian? Jesus very clearly stated that His followers will be recognized by the love they demonstrate for one another. It is obvious to me that any person who hates does not know or demonstrate the love of Jesus.

Paul D. Miller, professor of the practice of international affairs at Georgetown University and a research fellow with the Ethics and Religious Liberty Commission wrote an article that appeared in the February 3, 2021 edition of *Christianity Today.* The article was titled *What Is Christian Nationalism?* He began the article by presenting a series of questions: What is Christian nationalism, and how is it different from Christianity? How is it different from patriotism? How should Christians think about nations, especially about the United States? If nationalism is bad, does that mean we should reject nationality and national loyalty altogether?

Prof. Miller's description of Christian nationalism "Is the belief that the American nation is defined by Christianity, and that the government should take active steps to keep it that way". I do not agree with his assertion that Christian nationalists do not reject the First Amendment because they do. I believe what they do want is theocracy even though they would never admit it. I do agree with his observation that American Christians believe they should enjoy a privileged position in the public square. They also project a self-righteous attitude and consider themselves better than non-Christians. But these should never be the attitudes characteristic of authentic followers of Jesus Christ!

Andrew L. Whitehead and Samuel L Perry conducted a sociological study in which they gathered data through surveys and individual interviews and published the results of their study in their book, *Taking America Back For God: Christian Nationalism.* From their analysis of the collected data, they were able to summarize the ideology of Christian nationalists according to their agreement with the following six statements in **bold** followed by my response to each statement.

1. **The federal government should declare the United States a Christian nation.**

   This idea opposes the First Amendment of the US Constitution which states "Congress shall make no law respecting an establishment of religion, or prohibiting the free exercise thereof; or abridging the freedom of speech, or of the press; or the right of the people peaceably to assemble, and to petition the Government for a redress of grievances". This statement reveals that the aim of Christian nationalism is a system of government in which a religious body holds unlimited power.

2. **The federal government should advocate Christian values.**

   This statement also reveals that Christian nationalism aims to make all Americans practice the Christian religion. I grew up in a Pentecostal church at a time when women were forbidden from wearing lipstick or pants among many other trifling restrictions. Who gets to define Christian values, what is the biblical basis for defining Christian values, and how will they be enforced? Will there be morality police much like what Iran has imposed upon its citizens?

3. **The federal government should not enforce the strict separation of church and state.**

   Do Christian nationalists expect the First Amendment of the US Constitution to be repealed or modified?

4. **The federal government should allow religious symbols in public spaces.**

   The naivete of Christian nationalists is pathetic. The public display of religious symbols such as the Ten Commandments, the nativity scene, wearing a cross around one's neck, or displaying a cross, etc. does not make anyone or any nation Christian. Does this explain why a mob of Trump supporters, many sporting Christian signs, slogans, or symbols, believed it was their religious right to riot and storm the US Capitol building on January 6, 2021?

5. **The success of the United States is part of God's plan.**

    This idea is ludicrous. Exactly where in scripture is God's plan for the United States mentioned or even alluded to? By the way, the God of the Bible is not mentioned in the US Constitution.

6. **The federal government should allow prayer in public schools**.

    I discovered the most compelling scripture-based argument against Christian nationalism is presented by Andrew L. Seidel, a self-proclaimed atheist, in his book *The Founding Myth: Why Christian Nationalism Is Un-American*. Seidel uses Mathew 6:6 in his argument against government prayer, "But when you pray, go into your most private room, close the door and pray to your Father who is in secret, and your Father who sees [what is done] in secret will reward you."

    Jesus makes it very clear that public prayer is hypocritical and advises his followers they should pray in private. Throughout the four gospels, I read that Jesus pulled away to pray in private to Father God. I have not yet found in scripture where Jesus led a public prayer whenever people gathered to hear Him teach. So why do Christian nationalists demand laws that public praying should be allowed? I am so glad that nothing can prevent me from talking to Father God anytime and anywhere I want to. Besides, my prayers are for no one else's ears but God's.

The Rationale for Christian Nationalism

The messaging of Christian nationalism has no connection to the Gospel of Jesus Christ. Apostle Paul was extremely upset that the Galatians perverted the gospel of Christ into something contrary to what he taught them. I believe the ideology of Christian nationalism promotes a perversion of the Gospel that Apostle Paul spoke of in Galatians 1:6-9:

> [6] I am astonished *and* extremely irritated that you are so quickly shifting your allegiance *and* deserting Him who called you by the grace of Christ, for a different [even contrary] gospel; [7] which is really not another [gospel]; but there are [obviously] [b]some [people masquerading as teachers] who are disturbing *and* confusing you [with misleading, counterfeit teaching] and want to distort the gospel of Christ [twisting it into something which it is not]. [8] But even if we, or an angel from heaven, should preach to you a gospel contrary to that which we [originally] preached to you, let him be condemned to destruction! [9] As we have said before, so I now say again, if anyone is preaching to you a gospel different from that which you received [from us], let him be condemned to destruction!

Yes, I agree with Paul that Christian nationalism should be condemned! The messaging and belief system of Christian nationalism at no time includes Jesus' message of love and the Truth that sets us free from the bondage of sin. Instead, it seems that Christian nationalists have an inordinate fascination and attraction to lies. It is as though they have been hypnotized into joining a cult and blindly embracing its beliefs and practices. I believe Jesus would say to Christian nationalists the same thing He said in John 8:44:

> "**You are of *your* father the devil**, and it is your will to practice the desires [which are characteristic] of your

father. He was a murderer from the beginning and does not stand in the truth because there is no truth in him. When he lies, he speaks what is natural to him, **for he is a liar and the father of lies** *and* **half-truths."**

Jesus very clearly states in this verse that those who lie are like their father, the devil, who is the father of lies. Former President Trump was known and even celebrated for his incessant lies. The following is an excerpt from an article that appeared in the Washington Post:

> When The Washington Post Fact Checker team first started cataloging President Donald Trump's false or misleading claims, we recorded 492 suspect claims in the first 100 days of his presidency. On Nov. 2 alone, the day before the 2020 vote, Trump made 503 false or misleading claims as he barnstormed across the country in a desperate effort to win reelection. This astonishing jump in falsehoods is the story of Trump's tumultuous reign. By the end of his term, Trump had accumulated 30,573 untruths during his presidency — averaging about 21 erroneous claims a day.

How absurd that there are people engaged in a profession that tracts the lies of public figures? Living in America under Donald Trump's presidency was like living through a modern-day version of Hans Christian Anderson's *The Emperor's New Clothes*. It is the tale of a king who sets off in a procession before the whole city to show off his custom-designed "new clothes" and the townsfolk uncomfortably go along with the pretense, not wanting to appear inept or stupid, until a child blurts out that the emperor is wearing nothing at all. The people then realize that everyone has been fooled. Although startled, the emperor continues the procession, walking more proudly than ever. While one segment of Americans is mesmerized by Trump's boastful lies just like the townsfolk who appear inept and stupid, another segment is dumfounded like the little child who blurts out that the emperor is wearing no clothes.

Is it possible that Christian leaders who support Trump's lies are the false prophets Jesus warned of in Chapter 24 of the Gospel of Matthew? [11] "Many false prophets will appear and mislead many. [12] Because lawlessness is increased, the love of most people will grow cold."

What many American politicians declare to be law and order is lawlessness. American Christians appear to have the same religious bigoted attitude Paul had before he met Jesus on the road to Damascus. Before his encounter with Jesus, he was a devoutly religious Jew and a vigilante for enforcing the Hebrew laws even willing to kill those who failed to comply. The salvation that Jesus offers can never be obtained or enforced through legislation. It is amazing how Paul's encounter with Jesus transformed his heart from inflicting pain upon others to suffering pain for the cause of Christ as he expressed in 2 Corinthians 4:15, "These sufferings of ours are for your benefit. And the more of you who are won to Christ, the more there is to thank him for his great kindness, and the more the Lord is glorified."

Authentic followers of Jesus do not seek privilege and exclusivity but willingly serve others with the love, grace, and mercy of Jesus which is the essence of true Christianity that is missing from the messaging of Christian nationalism. Their ideology has been irritating my spirit for many years and I have spent much time seeking an explanation from God in scripture and prayer, but I am unable to reconcile Christian nationalism with the teachings of Jesus. I find that Christian nationalism repels people from Christ rather than draws them to Christ. Over the years I have heard many people who claim to be anointed prophets, evangelists, teachers, and apostles say things that do not line up with the teachings of Jesus. However, I do not want to be so critical of others that I end up throwing out the baby with the bathwater.

In my quest to learn about Christian nationalism, I discovered a plethora of books, articles, and videos on the topic. It was indeed refreshing to finally hear a white minister acknowledge and preach against the propaganda of Christian nationalism! Although many were written during and after Donald Trump's presidency, I also discovered many that were written years before Trump's election. Some were authored by Christians and some were authored by very credible non-Christians.

One book that I found profoundly impactful is *The Myth Of A Christian Nation* by Dr. Gregory A. Boyd, Senior Pastor of Woodland Hills Church in St. Paul, Minnesota, and President of Reknew.org. He shared that "in April of 2004, as the religious buzz was escalating, I felt it necessary to preach a series of sermons that would provide a biblical explanation for why our church should not join the rising chorus of right-wing political activity. I also decided this would be a good opportunity to expose the danger of associating the Christian faith too closely with any political point of view, whether conservative or liberal." (p. 9)

Dr. Boyd's thesis was that he believes a significant segment of American evangelicalism is guilty of nationalistic and political idolatry and I concur with his statement:

> Rather than focusing our understanding of God's kingdom on the person of Jesus—who, incidentally, never allowed himself to get pulled into the political disputes of his day— I believe many American evangelicals have allowed our understanding of the kingdom of God to be polluted with political ideals, agendas, and issues. (p. 11)

I emphatically agree with the following statement of Dr. Boyd, "Many Christians believe that America is, or at least once was, a Christian nation. We have argued that this notion is inaccurate for the simple reason that Christian means 'Christlike' and there never was a time when America as a nation acted Christlike." (p. 107)

Whenever I hear Christian friends complain about how

America has changed from what it was like when we were kids when prayer was allowed in school and people had respect for the Ten Commandments I want to scream! The notion that America is a Christian nation is bogus. In the pursuit of the American dream, Americans have committed hate-filled crimes against the humanity of their citizens from the very beginning and continue to do so in the name of Christian nationalism.

Dr. Boyd made an excellent point in raising the following questions:

> Did Jesus ever suggest by word or by example that we should aspire to acquire, let alone take over, the power of Caesar? Did Jesus spend any time and energy trying to improve, let alone dominate, the reigning government of his day? Did he ever work to pass laws against the sinners he hung out with and ministered to? Did he worry at all about ensuring that his rights and the religious rights of his followers were protected? Does any author in the New Testament remotely hint that engaging in this sort of activity has anything to do with the kingdom of God? The answer to all these questions is, of course, no. (p. 92)

On Monday, July 18, 2022, MSNBC host Rachel Maddow shared a video of Gerald L.K. Smith, a preacher, politician, and Nazi sympathizer who ran against Franklin Delano Roosevelt for president in 1944 on the *America First* ticket and founded what he coined as *Christian Nationalism*. The following are excerpts from a speech in which Smith spewed his ideological venom:

> We must keep control of our own money and our own blood. In other words, we must remain true to the Declaration of Independence. That is nationalism.
>
> We believe that the spiritual symbol of our statesmanship is the Cross, which indeed is the symbol

of Christianity.

Fight mongrelization and all attempts being made to force the intermixture of the black and white races.

Preserve America as a Christian Nation, being conscious of the fact that there is a highly organized campaign to substitute Jewish tradition for Christian tradition.

Jim Crow and white supremacy were in full effect in America during the 40s but Smith failed to attract many followers to Christian nationalism. In the 1944 Presidential election, Smith only garnered 1,781 votes. In his second bid for the presidency in 1956, he received eight write-in votes in California. After moving to Michigan, Smith ran for the United States Senate as a Republican but lost in the primary. His biographer, Glen Jeansonne, wrote, "Gerald Smith ran for president because he lusted for power, but his hatred for Jews and his relentless crusade against them had no such 'rational' motivation... Smith was fascinated by the Office of the President of the United States."

How ironic that Smith possessed the same irrational motivation and lust for power characteristic of former President Donald Trump who is now promoting Christian nationalism to regain the presidency. At an event Saturday, July 23, 2022, in Tampa, Florida, held by Turning Point USA, Trump said during a speech that "Americans kneel to God" alone, which is the concept of Christian nationalism that continues to gain traction among conservatives.

Smith only had a few hundred followers in the forties but here we are in 2022 and Trump has millions of followers! Katherine Stewart, journalist, and author of *The Power Worshippers: Inside the Dangerous Rise of Religious Nationalism* in an interview on CNN explained how former President Trump helped with the rise of Christian nationalism in US politics. She also stated that the goal of Christian nationalist leaders is conquest and division. Obviously, they are succeeding because there has not been such divisiveness in America since the Civil War!

I thought much progress has been made through the passage of the 1964 Civil Rights Act, the Voting Rights Act of 1965, and other progressive legislation to correct so many of America's social ills. Perhaps there never has been true progress but rather an illusion of progress. Sadly, hatred will never be irradicated by legislation.

Thinking that a Christian nation can be established in this fallen world is pointless and a myth-based ideology. Jesus never killed people to acquire political freedom for himself or others. Instead, He sacrificed His life on the cross not to condemn us but to free us from the bondage of sin and to gift us with eternal life (John 3:16-17). Contrary to the mantra of Christian nationalism America is not the promised land nor the city on a hill. When I hear Americans declare that America is the greatest and most powerful nation in the world I hear arrogance, pridefulness, elitism, selfishness, white supremacy, and hate. What mystifies me is that many who claim to be pro-life are so exclusively focused on the unborn that they fail to share the same compassion for the children that are born.

God has no favorite nation and His love for humankind has no boundaries which Apostle Paul explained in his letter to the Colossian church in Col. 3:10-12:

> [10] Each of you is now a new person. You are becoming more and more like your Creator, and you will understand him better. [11] **It doesn't matter if you are a Greek or a Jew**, or if you are circumcised or not. **You may even be a barbarian or a Scythian,[a] and you may be a slave or a free person. Yet Christ is all that matters, and he lives in all of us.** [12] God loves you and has chosen you as his own special people. So be gentle, kind, humble, meek, and patient.

Paul informed the church that every believer in Jesus Christ is born again into the Kingdom of God and citizens in God's Kingdom are not distinguished or segregated according to social status, skin color, ethnicity, gender, culture, or church membership. God loves every citizen of His Kingdom equally and we are in the process of developing the attributes and qualities that Jesus demonstrated when He lived on earth. As we follow Jesus' example, our interaction with fellow Americans should be gentle, kind, meek, and patient.

Christian nationalism has no place in America or any other nation. Instead, I recommend that American Christians seek after the Kingdom of God as described in Mark 4:11-12. The mystery of the kingdom of God will be revealed to true believers who have teachable hearts and are not gullible to the nonsense of Christian nationalism whereas the spiritually blind will continue to be drawn to the lies of Satan spread by Christian nationalism talking points.

Consider also Jesus' response to the man in Mark 10:17-31 when he asked Jesus what must he do to have eternal life. Jesus asked him if he obeyed the commandments and the man answered he faithfully obeyed them since he was a young man. The Amplified translation of Mark 10:21 records:

> Looking at him, Jesus felt a love (high regard, compassion) for him, and He said to him, "You lack one thing: go and sell all your property and give [the money] to the poor, and you will have [abundant] treasure in heaven; and come, follow Me [becoming My disciple, believing and trusting in Me and walking the same path of life that I walk].

However, Mark 10:22 records that the man was saddened at Jesus' words, and he left grieving because he owned much property and had many possessions which he treasured more than his relationship with God. Is it plausible that Christian nationalists treasure their "rights and privileges" of American citizenship, which are temporary, more than the eternal riches of citizenship in the Kingdom of God?

What is the rationale for Christian nationalism? There is none other than it is another tactic of the antichrist spirit which according to Eschatologist Dr. Curtis Dodson is on a mission to ""distort, marginalize, minimize, demean, cloud, disrupt, dishonor, demote, bring down, or misrepresent the image of Christ, His Church, or His message of love to the world."

7 Christian and Conservative

Labels, labels, labels! We are bombarded daily with labels and ideologies used to promote, put down, categorize, or otherwise describe people, especially regarding religion and politics. What I find most disturbing is the rhetoric from those who identify as Christians. There are so many labels being tossed in the airwaves that I find my head spinning daily! Labels such as right-leaning, left-leaning, patriotic, racist, progressive, woke, Democrat, and Republican are just a few that trigger such a visceral impact every day both in private conversations and on social media. What is newsworthy about the inane tweets by celebrities being lifted as news headlines? What is newsworthy in broadcasting the nonstop mindless commentary of crass media mouthpieces? Why are twitter opinions valued more than facts and truth? Father God is not the author of confusion, according to 1 Corinthians 14:33, but the god of confusion is enjoying a heyday!

For many years, I have heard the labels *conservative* and *liberal* tossed about. When I hear these labels used, they are often conflated with politics and religion. Whether in the media or general conversations, *liberalism* tends to have a negative connotation and *conservativism* tends to have a positive connotation. But whenever I hear the use of these terms causing so much controversy and confusion, I seek God's wisdom to gain His perspective on what is going on in the world today.

Liberal

When I look at scripture, *liberal* has a very positive connotation and appears throughout both the Old Testament and the New Testament. *Liberal* in Isaiah translates from the Hebrew *nadib* which means inclined, generous, and willing-hearted. In Proverbs *liberal* translates from the Hebrew *berakah* which means a blessing. In 2 Corinthians *liberal* translates from the Greek *haplotés* which is used to express singleness, i.e. (subjectively) sincerity (without dissimulation or self-seeking), or (objectively) generosity (copious bestowal) -- bountifulness, liberal, liberality, simplicity, or singleness. The biblical use of *liberal* agrees with the dictionary definition which implies that liberal is all about generosity and freedom from prejudice and bigotry.

The following statement was extracted from the article, *Christian Conservative*, by David W. Heughins (ProfDave), Adjunct Professor of History at Nazarene Bible College:

> What about Christian conservatives? HOLD IT!! There is nothing specifically conservative about being a Christian or specifically Christian about being a conservative. In context, Jesus was clearly a liberal! His feet were firmly planted in the Tanakh – the old covenant – but He instituted a *new* covenant in His blood. The Christian Bible includes both an Old and a *New* Testament. We say the Old is in the New revealed, the New is in the Old concealed. But Jesus was not crucified for being conservative.

Jesus is all about generosity and freedom from prejudice and bigotry. Jesus' perspective of *liberalism* is very positive. As a disciple of Jesus, I completely identify with being *liberal* just like Jesus!

Conservatism

When searching scripture for *conservative* I could find it nowhere in the Bible. I recall hearing a speech from former Vice President Mike Pence in which he proudly proclaimed himself "Christian and conservative". Since I could find no reference to *conservativism* in the Bible, I began to search the Internet for a definition. The Wikipedia website provides the following:

> *Conservatism* is an aesthetic, cultural, social,

and political philosophy, which seeks to promote and preserve *traditional* social institutions. The central tenets of *conservatism* may vary on the status quo of the culture and civilization in which it appears.
In Western culture, *conservatives* seek to preserve a range of institutions such as organized religion, parliamentary government, and property rights. Adherents of *conservatism* often oppose progressivism and seek a return to *traditional* values.

Merriam-Webster dictionary provides the following definition of *conservatism*:

1. a: disposition in politics to preserve what is established b: a political philosophy based on *tradition* and social stability, stressing established institutions, and preferring gradual development to abrupt change
2. the tendency to prefer an existing or *traditional* situation to change

As I continued my search for a definition of *conservatism*, I discovered many other labels attached to *conservatism* such as social *conservatism*, religious *conservatism*, and cultural conservatism. Religious *conservatism* principally applies the teachings of particular religions to politics: sometimes by merely proclaiming the value of those teachings and at other times, by having those teachings influence laws. In most democracies, political *conservatism* seeks to uphold *traditional* family structures and social values. Religious *conservatives* typically oppose abortion, LGBTQ behavior (or, in certain cases, identity), drug use, and sexual activity outside of marriage. In some cases, *conservative* values are grounded in religious beliefs, and *conservatives* seek to increase the role of religion in public life.

Of course, to some religious *conservatism* may appear noble and morally correct, but insisting upon making and enforcing laws against immorality was not how Jesus transformed lives! Dr. Gregory A. Boyd, Senior Pastor of Woodland Hills Church in St. Paul, Minnesota, and President of Reknew.org said it best in his book, *The Myth of A Christian Nation:*

> Did Jesus spend any time and energy trying to improve, let alone dominate, the reigning government of his day? Did he ever work to pass laws against the sinners he hung out with and ministered to? Did he worry at all about ensuring that his rights and the religious rights of his followers were protected? Does any author in the New Testament remotely hint that engaging in this sort of activity has anything to do with the kingdom of God? The answer to all these questions is, of course, no. (p. 92)

Thank you, Dr. Boyd, for confirming my hypothesis!

Tradition

One word that stood out to me in both the definitions and descriptions of *conservativism,* is the word *tradition. Tradition* is the one word I find in the Bible where Jesus told us exactly what He thinks about it in the following texts:

Matthew 15:3 - "Why also do you violate the commandment of God for the sake of your *tradition* [handed down by the elders]?"

Matthew 15:6 – "So by this, you have invalidated the word of God [depriving it of force and authority and making it of no effect] for the sake of your *tradition* [handed down by the elders]."

Mark 7:9 – "You are experts at setting aside *and* nullifying the commandment of God to keep your [man-made] *tradition and* regulations."

Mark 7:13 – "so you nullify the [authority of the] word of God [acting as if it did not apply] because of your *tradition* which you have handed down [through the elders]. And you do many things such as that."

Merriam-Webster dictionary provides the following definition of *tradition*:
1. a: an inherited, established, or customary pattern of thought, action, or behavior (such as a religious practice or a social custom) b: a belief or story or body of beliefs or stories relating to the past that are commonly accepted as historical though not verifiable
2. the handing down of information, beliefs, and customs by word of mouth or by example from one generation to another without written instruction
3. cultural continuity in social attitudes, customs, and institutions
4. characteristic manner, method, or style

I think Jesus made very clear his contempt for man-made *traditions*. And I think it is safe to conclude that He considers Christian *conservatism* equally contemptible. American Christianity is entrenched in *tradition* that insists upon maintaining a status quo that is deeply anchored in the following premises:

1. male domination over all sectors of government and social matters
2. financial control dominated by the wealthy class
3. white supremacy dominates over all other people groups

When the Founding Fathers composed the US Constitution, Bill of Rights, and Declaration of Independence, they were not concerned about anyone other than the wealthy male landowners of their time. Their purview did not include women, the native people of this land, poor whites who did not own land, nor the enslaved Africans who made these men wealthy working the land stolen from the native people.

When Patrick Henry declared, "Give me liberty or give me death" he did not even consider liberating the many humans he owned as property. General Washington fought valiantly to gain freedom from the tyranny of British King George, but as president, he never freed the hundreds of enslaved Africans that kept his plantations thriving. Benjamin Franklin, with all his brilliance in scientific discoveries, failed to recognize the humanity of the enslaved Africans when he audaciously stated, "Why to increase the Sons of *Africa*, by planting them in *America*, where we have so fair an Opportunity, by excluding all Blacks and Tawneys, of increasing the lovely White and Red?" Thomas Jefferson may have written "all men are created equal" yet he enslaved more than 600 human beings over the course of his life. Yet, American Christians love to venerate the Founding Fathers from their pulpits every July during their Independence Day celebration.

Tradition in the New Testament translates from the Greek word paradosis, defined in Strong's Concordance as handing down or over, a *tradition*. The Jews derived their man-made *traditions* from their feeble attempt to obey the laws of the Hebrew Bible. When the Pharisees asked Jesus, "What is the most important commandment in the Law?" He replied:

> [37] 'YOU SHALL LOVE THE LORD YOUR GOD WITH ALL YOUR HEART, AND WITH ALL YOUR SOUL, AND WITH ALL YOUR MIND.' [38] This is the first and greatest commandment. [39] The second is like it, 'YOU SHALL LOVE YOUR NEIGHBOR AS YOURSELF [that is, unselfishly seek the best or higher good for others].' [40] The whole Law and the [writings of the] Prophets depend on these two commandments." (Matthew 22:37-40)

Jesus succinctly explained that compliance with God's commandments cannot be accomplished without first recognizing His love for us. God is love and He created every life to be in a loving relationship with Him. Our very existence is dependent upon His love, whether we believe in Him or not. When we truly understand His love for us and establish a relationship with Him as Father God, everything we say or do should be motivated by His love. The result of our love relationship with God is that we can love ourselves and others the same way God loves us. When we love God with all our heart, soul, and mind it will manifest in our lives according to 1 Corinthians 13:4 – 8:

> Love never gives up.
> Love cares more for others than for self.
> Love doesn't want what it doesn't have.
> Love doesn't strut,
> Doesn't have a swelled head,
> Doesn't force itself on others,
> Isn't always "me first,"
> Doesn't fly off the handle,
> Doesn't keep score of the sins of others,
> Doesn't revel when others grovel,
> Takes pleasure in the flowering of truth,
> Puts up with anything,
> Trusts God always,
> Always looks for the best,
> Never looks back, but keeps going to the end.

I learned in grade school to recite *The Pledge of Allegiance* every day at the beginning of class. However, the phrase "One nation, under God, indivisible, with liberty and justice for all" will never be realized in America without the love of God in the heart, soul, and mind of every American!

Former President Donald Trump and followers of Christian nationalism may shout they want to "make America great again". But I prefer the sentiments expressed by my favorite African American poet, social activist, novelist, and playwright, Langston Hughes. The following are excerpts from his magnificent poem, *Let America Be America Again*:

Let America be America again.
Let it be the dream it used to be.
Let it be the pioneer on the plain
Seeking a home where he himself is free.
(America never was America to me.)

O, let my land be a land where Liberty
Is crowned with no false patriotic wreath,
But opportunity is real, and life is free,
Equality is in the air we breathe.
(There's never been equality for me,
Nor freedom in this "homeland of the free.")

I am the poor white, fooled and pushed apart,
I am the Negro bearing slavery's scars.
I am the red man driven from the land,
I am the immigrant clutching the hope I seek—
And finding only the same old stupid plan
Of dog eat dog, of mighty crush the weak.

O, let America be America again—
The land that never has been yet—
And yet must be—the land where *every* man is free.
The land that's mine—the poor man's, Indian's, Negro's, ME—
Who made America,
Whose sweat and blood, whose faith and pain,
Whose hand at the foundry, whose plow in the rain,
Must bring back our mighty dream again.

Love Trumps Tradition

It is obvious to me Christian *conservatives* are modern-day Pharisees. How ironic it was that the only people that constantly opposed the teachings of Jesus were the Pharisees and many Jewish leaders. Although their lives were dedicated to studying and teaching the Hebrew

Bible or Tanak and were zealous in enforcing the Hebrew law as presented in the Torah (Pentateuch or the Five Books of Moses), they failed to recognize that Jesus was the Messiah prophesied about in the writings of the Prophets. I suspect that Jesus is lamenting over Christian *conservatives* today just as He did in ancient times over the Jews in Matthew 23:37:

> O Jerusalem, Jerusalem, who murders the prophets and stones [to death] those [messengers] who are sent to her [by God]! How often I wanted to gather your children together [around Me], as a hen gathers her chicks under her wings, and you were unwilling.

I imagine if Jesus were to address Christian *conservatives* today it may sound something like this:

> Oh, Bible-toting, scripture-quoting, tongue-talking self-proclaimed Christians, instead of throwing stones at and driving away non-Christians you should be letting your light shine and drawing them to Me, by sharing My love with them. I long to embrace them in my love but your self-righteous and bigoted attitude is repelling them away from me.

Before Paul met Jesus on the road to Damascus, he was staunchly devoted to enforcing obedience to the *traditions* imposed by Hebrew law. Paul shared his Jewish pedigree in Philippians chapter 3:4-10. Before his encounter with Jesus, Paul could boast of his status as a "Hebrew of Hebrews" because he faithfully adhered to the *traditions* of the Jewish religion. He took pride in how he persecuted the followers of Jesus as his right to defend the Jewish faith. He dared to think he was doing God a favor and expecting a pat on the back for his zealous defense of the faith! But then he met Jesus! In the Living Bible Translation of Verses 9 and 10, Paul sums it up best when he said:

> [9] I become one with him, no longer counting on being saved by being good enough or by obeying God's laws,

but by trusting Christ to save me; for God's way of making us right with himself depends on faith—counting on Christ alone. ¹⁰ Now I have given up everything else—I have found it to be the only way to really know Christ and to experience the mighty power that brought him back to life again, and to find out what it means to suffer and to die with him.

The epiphany that Paul experienced with Jesus on the road to Damascus produced Apostle Paul whose writings eventually became thirteen books of the New Testament. Paul's transformation assures us that there is hope for the religious *conservatives* and religious *traditionalists* of today! Simply one authentic encounter with Jesus can transform their hearts and minds and empower them to manifest the love of Jesus. Instead of persecuting people that they consider outcasts (non-Christians, LGBTQ, immigrants from "s##t hole" nations, pro-abortionists, homeless, imprisoned, drug abusers, poor, etc.) they can begin to love their neighbor the way that God loves them. Jesus declared, "And I, if *and* when I am lifted up from the earth [on the cross], will draw all *people* to Myself [Gentiles, as well as Jews]." (John 12:32) When we *liberally* share the love, grace, and mercy of Jesus, it will draw people to God by the millions – that is His ultimate desire for all humankind!

To be an authentic Christian one must be committed to sharing the love of Jesus. To be conservative implies one is committed to *traditions* that deny the love of Jesus. Is it possible to be both Christ-like and conservative? According to Jesus, I think not!

8 The Antichrist Spirit

The Gospel of Jesus Christ has been hijacked by the antichrist spirit in the messaging and actions of many Americans who identify as Christians. Instead of spreading the Good News of the gift of salvation offered by Jesus Christ, certain Christians have been seduced into promoting religion and the culture of religion. Rather than introducing non-believers to a loving relationship with God through His son Jesus Christ, American Christians think that imposing and enforcing a set of laws and regulations will make a person an acceptable Christian. But God's love is "missing in the action" among too many Americans who declare themselves Christian. Why would Christians cause so much hate, discord, and divisiveness throughout America?

The antichrist spirit is the source of hate-mongering in America. You may ask, "Exactly what is the antichrist spirit?" and "How is it possible for Americans who identify as Christians to be both Christian and at the same time antichrist?" First of all, anti- is a prefix that implies opposition or hostility to the word it precedes. Simply stated the antichrist spirit opposes and is hostile to Jesus Christ, the only begotten son of God. Dr. Curtis Dodson, highly respected eschatologist and Chancellor of The WordWise Institute of Eschatology provided the following definition/description of the antichrist spirit: *"Any actions, words, deeds, or behaviors that distort, marginalize, minimize, demean, cloud, disrupt, dishonor, demote, bring down, or misrepresent the image of Christ, His Church, or His message of love to the world."*

Dr. Dodson's description of the antichrist spirit correlates with the thief described in John 10:10 who comes only to steal, kill, and destroy. The antichrist spirit is on a mission to prevent humankind, God's most beloved creation, from fulfilling God's purpose which is to redeem and restore us to the Father-child relationship that He created us for. The antichrist spirit attempts to destroy human beings, by any means necessary, and sadly many Americans who identify as Christian are aiding and abetting the antichrist spirit.

Politics and religion are complicit strange bedfellows and both are used by the antichrist spirit to *distort, marginalize, minimize, demean, cloud, disrupt, dishonor, demote, bring down, or misrepresent the image of Christ, His Church, or His message of love to the world.* The only ones who opposed Jesus and His teachings were the religious leaders. He constantly had run-ins with certain Jews known as Pharisees, Sadducees, and priests. They challenged Jesus for not complying with Hebrew laws such as keeping the Sabbath (Matthew 12:2) and stoning the woman who was caught in adultery (John 8:3-11). In Matthew 23:33 Jesus explained that the serpent was used by Satan to introduce evil into the Garden of Eden (Genesis 3) and Satan was the serpent working through the religious leaders to continue the propagation of evil through deception, false teaching, and man-made laws and traditions which were given priority over God's law.

The Jewish chief priests and elders plotted to arrest and kill Jesus (Matthew 26:3-4). But they had to appeal to the political leaders of the Roman Empire and convince them to permit the crucifixion of Jesus. Pilate, the governor of Judea, protested three times to the Jewish leaders that He found no fault in Jesus before he finally acquiesced to their demand that He be crucified (John 18:38, 19:4,6).

It was the antichrist spirit that instigated the Jewish leaders to demand the crucifixion of Jesus and it is the antichrist spirit that is instigating many American religious leaders of today to promote the passage of laws to make America a Christian nation. Satan continues to use religious people to point accusing fingers at unchurched and secular people as the cause of evil in society. However, religious people continue to oppose Jesus' teachings on love, grace, and mercy even today. You will find the religious filling the church pews every Sunday serving as deacons, ushers, choir members, Sunday school teachers, and even pastors who vigorously insist that

America must return to being a Christian nation.

Christian nationalism is a tactic of the antichrist spirit to make America officially a Christian nation and is growing in popularity every day. However, I have read the Gospels of Matthew, Mark, Luke, and John many times and have yet to find one instance where Jesus ever even suggested that His gift of salvation is obtainable through national identity or religious affiliation. Nowhere in scripture did Jesus give the disciples instructions to make disciples through legislation!
Apostle John made it very clear in 2 John 1:7 that it is religious people posing as Christians that carry the antichrist spirit and are therefore antagonists of Christ. "For **many deceivers [heretics, posing as Christians] have gone out into the world**, those who do not acknowledge *and* confess the coming of Jesus Christ in the flesh (bodily form). This [person, **the kind who does this] is the deceiver and the antichrist [that is, the antagonist of Christ]**." I have read and listened very carefully to the rhetoric of Christian nationalists and find it interesting that **they never mention the name of Jesus**!

How is it possible to proclaim to be a Christian without ever lifting the Name of Jesus? Apostle John answered this question in his letters to the early church. 1 John 2:22 states, "Who is the liar but the one who denies that Jesus is the Christ (the Messiah, the Anointed)? This is the **antichrist [the enemy and antagonist of Christ], the one who denies *and* consistently refuses to acknowledge the Father and the Son**." And 1 John 4:3 declares ".. **every spirit that does not confess Jesus [acknowledging that He has come in the flesh, but would deny any of Son's true nature] is not of God**; this is the *spirit* of the **antichrist**, which you have heard is coming and **is now already in the world**." Both scriptures clearly define the antichrist spirit as the enemy of Christ that consistently refuses to acknowledge Jesus as the son of God.

The proliferation of anger and divisiveness that exists in

America is not only in political and religious circles but even between friends and family members. A family member told me that her neighbor was so enraged that Donald Trump lost the 2020 election she had a heart attack. When she was discharged from the hospital her husband and son chose to have her placed in a nursing home rather than allow her to return home and receive home-based care. How sad that her life ended alone in a nursing home separated from her family.

There are news reports daily about wars going on all around the world, but these wars are not in the control of human flesh and blood. War declared by Russian dictator Putin upon Ukraine, the war in Iran against women, and all other wars are actually orchestrated by the spiritual *forces* of wickedness in the heavenly (supernatural) places explained by Apostle Paul to the church in 2 Corinthian 10:3 – 7:

> [3] For though we walk in the flesh [as mortal men], we are not carrying on our [spiritual] warfare according to the flesh *and* using the weapons of man. [4] **The weapons of our warfare are not physical [weapons of flesh and blood]. Our weapons are divinely powerful for the destruction of fortresses.** [5] ***We are* destroying sophisticated arguments and every exalted *and* proud thing that sets itself up against the [true] knowledge of God, and *we are* taking every thought *and* purpose captive to the obedience of Christ**, [6] being ready to punish every act of disobedience when your own obedience [as a church] is complete. [7] You are looking [only] at the outward appearance of things. If anyone is confident that he is Christ's, he should reflect *and* consider this, that **just as he is Christ's, so too are we.**

There are activities in the spiritual realm that impact what we experience in the physical realm. But no physical weapons (guns, atomic bombs, missiles, arguments, sanctions, etc.) are suitable for spiritual warfare. Ephesians 6:10-12 describe how God provides His people with appropriate weapons to guarantee victory in our battle with Satan:

> **¹⁰ In conclusion, be strong in the Lord [draw your strength from Him and be empowered through your union with Him] and in the power of His [boundless] might. ¹¹ Put on the full armor of God [for His precepts are like the splendid armor of a heavily-armed soldier], so that you may be able to [successfully] stand up against all the schemes** *and* **the strategies** *and* **the deceits of the devil. ¹² For our struggle is not against flesh and blood [contending only with physical opponents], but against the rulers, against the powers, against the world forces of this [present] darkness, against the spiritual** *forces* **of wickedness in the heavenly (supernatural)** *places.*

Jesus was constantly attacked by Satan and every believer in Jesus who has received His gift of salvation can learn from Jesus how to overcome the attacks of Satan. In the Message translation of the Gospel of John 16:31-33 Jesus shared the following with the disciples:

> ³¹⁻³³ Jesus answered them, "Do you finally believe? In fact, you're about to make a run for it—saving your own skins and abandoning me. But I'm not abandoned. The Father is with me. I've told you all this so that **trusting me, you will be unshakable and assured, deeply at peace. In this godless world, you will continue to experience difficulties. But take heart! I've conquered the world."**

You may ask, "How can I be at peace amid all the madness in this godless world?" Jesus says trusting Him assures us that His presence in our lives enables us to conquer the world right along with Him! 1 John 4:4 affirms, "Little children (believers, dear ones), you are of God *and* you belong to Him and have [already] overcome them [the agents of the **antichrist**]; because **He (Jesus) who is in you is greater**

than he (Satan) who is in the world [of sinful mankind]." The following table is a short list of Satan's war arsenal contrasted with the arsenal that God gives us.

Spiritual Weapons of Warfare

Satan's Arsenal	God's Arsenal
1. From the beginning of time, **lies** and **deception** have been Satan's primary choice of weapons. This is the tactic he used when he convinced Adam and Eve to disobey God in the Garden of Eden. (Gen.3)	Jesus did not mince words when He exposed Satan as the father of lies. **Speaking the Truth is Jesus' weapon against lies and deception**. [44] You are of *your* father the devil, and it is your will to practice the desires [which are characteristic] of your father. He was a murderer from the beginning and does not stand in the truth because there is no truth in him. When he lies, he speaks what is natural to him, for **he is a liar and the father of lies *and* half-truths**. [45] But because I **speak the truth**, you do not believe Me [and continue in your unbelief]. (John 8:44-45)
2. The interpretation of the 2nd amendment to the US Constitution legalizes the proliferation of gun **violence**. There is a	Jesus never retaliated violence with violence. When Jesus was arrested in Gethsemane Peter fought back by

	significant number of Americans who value their "right to bear arms" over protecting innocent children from gun violence.	pulling out his sword and cutting the ear of the soldier. Jesus told Peter, "Put your sword back in its place; for all **those who *habitually* draw the sword will die by the sword**." The US Constitution may give Americans the right to bear arms but Jesus does not permit His followers to do so. Instead, He instructs us to [14] ***Continually* pursue peace** with everyone, and the sanctification without which no one will [ever] see the Lord. [15] **See to it that no one falls short of God's grace; that no root of resentment springs up and causes trouble**, and by it, many are defiled. (Hebrews 12:14-1).
3.	**White supremacy/racism** is the blatant and systematic denial of the human rights of non-white people in their pursuit of life, liberty, and happiness. **Genocide** is the deliberate and systematic destruction of a racial, political, or cultural group.	White supremacy, racism, and Genocide express nothing but pure hate. Jesus instructed His followers to respond to hate with love. He said, "But I say to you who hear [Me and pay attention to My words]: **Love [that is, unselfishly seek the best or higher good for]**

	your enemies, [make it a practice to] **do good to those who hate you,** ²⁸ bless *and* show kindness to those who curse you, **pray for those who mistreat you.**" (Luke 6:27-28) However, we must first receive the love of God before we can share the love with others. **Love the Lord with all your heart, and with all understanding, and with all your soul, and with all your strength, and to love your neighbor like yourself.** (Mark 12:33).
4. **Greed** values wealth and power over the value of human life. **Human trafficking** involves the capture and enslavement of innocent children and young women to fulfill the insatiable lust and greed of men	Greed is selfishness. "**Do nothing from selfishness or empty conceit** [through factional motives, or strife], but with [an attitude of] humility [being neither arrogant nor self-righteous], **regard others as more important than yourselves.**" (Philippians 2:3)
5. **Homophobia** is an irrational fear of, aversion to, or discrimination against homosexuality or gay people. **Xenophobia**	**Jesus never persecuted or ridiculed anyone for being sinful or different from** "normal" and neither

is fear, and hatred of strangers or foreigners or anything strange or foreign.	**should we**. He went out of His way to minister to the outcasts and marginalized of His day and we must follow His example.
6. **Misogyny** is hatred of, aversion to, or prejudice against women. This attitude promotes the continued abuse, persecution, and murder of women in America.	**Jesus welcomed women to follow Him** and many were numbered among His disciples. Jesus even went out of His way to minister to the Samaritan woman who was considered an outcast by the Jews. (John 4:4-30)
7. **Injustice** is the systematic resistance to the fair and just treatment of people of color by the US judicial system.	Christians are instructed to actively advocate for justice. "**Speak up for the people who have no voice, for the rights of all the misfits. Speak out for justice! Stand up for the poor and destitute!**" (Proverbs 31:8-9 - MSG)

Conclusion

Satan and the antichrist spirit are the same entity. Spiritual warfare is all about Satan thinking he can conquer God by destroying what God loves the most which are the human beings that He created in His image and likeness and for His glory (Genesis 1:26-27). Newsflash! Satan is no match for the omnipotent, omnipresent, and omniscient true and living God!

All authentic (not false or imitation) followers of Jesus should keep in mind the following words God declares over your life, especially when you feel overwhelmed and battle-weary:

- **⁹ Let us not grow weary *or* become discouraged in doing good, for at the proper time we will reap if we do not give in.** ¹⁰ So then, while we [as individual believers] have the opportunity, let us do good to all people [not only being helpful, but also doing that which promotes their spiritual well-being], and especially [be a blessing] to those of the household of faith (born-again believers). (Galatians 6:9-10)

- ¹⁹ My brothers and sisters, if anyone among you strays from the truth *and* falls into error and [another] one turns him back [to God], ²⁰ let the [latter] one know that **the one who has turned a sinner from the error of his way will save that one's soul from death and cover a multitude of sins** [that is, obtain the pardon of the many sins committed by the one who has been restored]. (James 5:19-20)

- ³¹ What then shall we say to all these things? **If God is for us, who can be [successful] against us?**

  ³⁷ Yet **in all these things we are more than conquerors** *and* gain an overwhelming victory through Him who loved us [so much that He died for us]. ³⁸ For I am convinced [and continue to be convinced—beyond any doubt] that **neither death, nor life, nor angels, nor principalities, nor things present *and* threatening, nor things to come, nor powers,** ³⁹ **nor height, nor depth, nor any other created thing, will be able to separate us from the [unlimited] love of God, which is in Christ Jesus our Lord.** (Romans 8:31, 37-39)

- **3-6** How blessed is God! And what a blessing he is! He's the Father of our Master, Jesus Christ, and takes us to the high places of blessing in him. **Long before he laid down earth's foundations, he had us in mind and had settled on us as the focus of his love, to be made whole and holy by his love. Long, long ago he decided to adopt us into his family through Jesus Christ. (What pleasure he took in planning this!) He wanted us to enter into the celebration of his lavish gift-giving by the hand of his beloved Son.** (Ephesians 1:3-6 - MSG)

AMEN!

9 Is American Christianity Antichrist? – Conclusion

My journey of discovery attempting to understand American Christianity as presented by Christian nationalism, Christian conservatism, and evangelicals has been a spiritual and emotional roller coaster ride – and I have never liked roller coaster rides! I believe my journey was initiated by the Christian ethics classes I took in seminary. These classes inspired me in my reading of the biblical text to do the following:

1) accurately hear what God is saying (Luke 8:8)

2) interpret and discern its messages as guided by the Holy Spirit (John 14:26)

3) circumspectly apply its principles in my life (Ephesians 5:15)

During my first semester in seminary, we were assigned to read *God's Long Summer: Stories of Faith and Civil Rights* authored by Charles Marsh. From reading his book I learned of the hatred and opposition white preachers had towards Dr. Martin Luther King Jr.'s quest for civil rights for blacks in America. I greatly appreciate the following review of Marsh's book that appears in the book cover by the late Congressman John Lewis:

> Without prayer- without a spiritual anchor – my involvement in the civil rights movement would have been like a bird without wings. Mississippi Freedom Summer tested my commitment and my faith. At times, I asked "Where is God? Did he forget his children?" To this day, I wonder how those who opposed us reconciled their faith with their hatred and anger or even their inaction. God's Long Summer admirably attempts to explore this unfathomable paradox.

Like Congressman Lewis, I too could not understand how anyone who claimed to be a Christian would oppose Rev. King's leadership in seeking civil and humane treatment for all citizens. And I am perplexed that this animosity still prevails in American Christianity in the 21st Century!

The ideology of American Christianity is unethical because it is not righteous and does not reflect the message of the love of Jesus and His gracious gift of salvation. Instead, it promotes self-righteousness, religious bigotry, judgementalism, exclusion, and the supremacy of one group of people over all others. It unquestionably promotes the spirit of the antichrist through lies and deception and opposes the grace and mercy that Jesus offers to all humankind.

Is it possible that God used the election of Donald Trump to the presidency of the United States of America to expose the hypocrisy of the American version of Christianity? Genesis 45 reveals how God used the mistreatment inflicted upon Joseph by his brothers to save his entire family from the threat of famine. Contrary to former President Trump's mantra to "Make America Great Again" I believe God used his election to expose the spiritual famine of American Christianity and the fact that America has never been great nor will it ever be great if it continues on its current course.

America has been engaged in a war against Muslim terrorism in the past few decades. But the fact is this: America was founded and established as a result of multiple terrorist acts perpetrated by European colonizers against the indigenous people who inhabited this land. But, of course, that is not the story told in the American historical narrative taught in American schools since the founding of this nation. American Christians have been guilty of spreading and preaching this lie from their pulpits even to this day. The results from the 2020 election revealed that the divisiveness among Americans is almost 50/50. Fifty percent believe the lie and fifty percent reject the lie. This is an indictment against

Christian nationalism for spreading lies rather than sharing the love of Jesus.

John 3:16 is one of the most quoted scriptures. But we fail to share the complete message if we omit John 3:17 which says, "God did not send the Son into the world to judge *and* condemn the world [that is, to initiate the final judgment of the world], but that the world might be saved through Him."

God did not inspire me to write this book to condemn or judge American Christians. His assignment for me is to remind us that God is more concerned with our redemption and restoration than with judgment and punishment. Consider the following six realizations about God's love for us:

1. **Do you realize that God's love for us is so extravagant that He refuses to live without us?**

   That is why He sent Jesus to die on the cross and pay the penalty for our sins so that He can enjoy being with us for all eternity. God demonstrated his love for us that while we were still sinners, Christ died for us (Romans 5:8). God's amazing grace is such a phenomenal expression of His profusely magnanimous unfailing love for us.

2. **Do you realize that Jesus paid the penalty for our sins even before we asked for forgiveness?**

   As He hung dying on the cross about to breathe His last breath, He interceded for us and asked, "Father, forgive them, for they do not know what they are doing" (Luke 23:34a).

3. **Do you realize that when Jesus was hanging on the cross and declared "It is finished", bowed his head, and died (John 19:30), all our sins - past,**

present, and future - were transferred from our account to His?

Why would Jesus pay the penalty for our sins before we were born? God's love for us is beyond human comprehension!

4. **Do you realize that when Jesus sacrificed His blood on Calvary for you and me He exonerated us from our sinful state and erased our sin from God's memory?**

In Hebrews 10:17-18 He declared, [17] "I will never again remember their sins and lawless deeds. [18] Now, when sins have once been forever forgiven and forgotten, there is no need to offer more sacrifices to get rid of them." If God refuses to remember our sins, then we have no reason to wallow in sin or point out or accuse others of their sins.

5. **Do you realize there is absolutely nothing that can stop God from loving us?**

Apostle Paul explained it best in Romans 8:38-39, [38] "I am convinced [and continue to be convinced—beyond any doubt] that neither death, nor life, nor angels, nor principalities, nor things present *and* threatening, nor things to come, nor powers, [39] nor height, nor depth, nor any other created thing, will be able to separate us from the [unlimited] love of God, which is in Christ Jesus our Lord."
That's right, no matter what we do and no matter what Satan does to us or even through us, God loves us anyway!

6. **Do you realize God's victory over Satan is guaranteed?**

Jesus declared in John 10:28-29 [28] "I give them eternal

life, and they shall never perish; no one will snatch them out of my hand. ²⁹ My Father, who has given them to me, is greater than all; **no one can snatch them out of my Father's hand**." How awesome it is that the lives of every believer in Jesus are in God's hands and there is no way He will allow Satan to snatch us out of His hands. Knowing this should make you want to shout and dance!

Redemption

Although American Christianity is grossly in error, I believe there is still hope. The corrective action is provided in the epistle of James. I especially appreciate the Message translation of James 5:19-20 which says,

> My dear friends, if you know people who have wandered off from God's truth, don't write them off. Go after them. Get them back and you will have rescued precious lives from destruction and prevented an epidemic of wandering away from God.

Those who have been ensnared by American Christianity and wandered off from God's truth simply need to turn back to the Truth in Jesus. It is knowing His Truth that will set you free (John 8:32). There is a saying "when you know better you do better". Now that you know better, you can begin to do better and live a life that honors God and blesses those with whom you come in contact (1 Peter 4:10).

Restoration

1 Peter 4:7-11 provides the remedy to restoring our relationship with God:

> ⁷⁻¹¹ Everything in the world is about to be wrapped up, so take nothing for granted. Stay wide awake in prayer. Most of all, love each other as if your life depended on it. Love makes up for practically anything. Be quick to

give a meal to the hungry, a bed to the homeless—cheerfully. Be generous with the different things God gave you, passing them around so all get in on it: if words, let it be God's words; if help, let it be God's hearty help. That way, God's bright presence will be evident in everything through Jesus, and *he'll* get all the credit as the One mighty in everything—encores to the end of time. Oh, yes!

Homelessness is an obvious crisis all across America today. Christians should not depend upon government leaders to properly address this issue. We, the people of God, can use our God-given resources to meet many of the needs of those who are socially, physically, and economically oppressed. We are admonished in James 1:27 to look after orphans and widows in their distress. Most buildings where church congregations gather are only occupied for a few hours a week and are vacant the majority of the time. God would be so honored and pleased if congregations would make their facilities available to provide shelter and meals to the homeless (Matthew 25:37-40). Also, church facilities can be used to provide a haven for children of single parents after school and during the summer and spring breaks. In addition, church facilities can be used to provide community-based mental health and social welfare services. These are just a few ways in which Christians can fulfill our calling to the ministry of reconciliation described in 2 Corinthians 5:18,"But all *these* things are from God, who reconciled us to Himself through Christ [making us acceptable to Him] and gave us the ministry of reconciliation [so that by our example we might bring others to Him]."

As authentic followers of Jesus, we have the awesome privilege of sharing His love, grace, and mercy with those yet under the influence of the prince of darkness: the antichrist spirit of Satan. We are empowered by the Holy Spirit to make a positive impact on the lives of everyone with whom we encounter daily. It can be as simple as a smile or a kind word. Instead of boasting about being a Christian, He wants us to

be change agents and demonstrate Christ-likeness by the way we treat one another. God is love and God created every life to receive His love which in turn frees us to love Him, to love ourselves, and to love our neighbors the same way God loves us. That is what Jesus requires of His authentic followers. The late psalmist Andrea Crouch best summed it up in a song he wrote – **Jesus is the answer for the world today, above Him, there's no other, Jesus is the way.**
Amen! Amen! Amen!

Bibliography

Note	Author/Source	Books/Articles/Videos
1	Robert P. Jones CEO Public Religion Research Institute (PRRI)	*The End of White Christian America* (July 12, 2016) ISBN 978-1-5011-2229-3 *White Too Long: The Legacy of White Supremacy in American Christianity*. (July 28, 2020) ISBN 978-1-9821-2286-7 https://www.prri.org/
2	Andrew L. Seidel	*The Founding Myth: Why Christian Nationalism Is Un-American* (2019) ISBN 978-1-4549-3327-4
3	Michelle Goldberg	*Kingdom Coming: The Rise of Christian Nationalism* (2006, 2007) ISBN 978-0-393-32976-6
4	Andrew L. Whitehead and Samuel L. Perry	*Taking America Back For God: Christian Nationalism in the United States* (2020) ISBN 978-0-19-005788-6
5	Anthea Butler	*White Evangelical Racism: The Politics of Morality in America* (2021) ISBN 978-1-4696-6117-9
6	Duke L. Kwon and Gregory Thompson	*Reparations: A Christian Call For Repentance and Repair* (2021) ISBN 978-1-58743-450-1
7	Kristin Kobes Du Mez	*Jesus and John Wayne: How White Evangelicals Corrupted a Faith and Fractured a Nation* (2020) ISBN 978-1-63149-905-0
8	Dr. Eddie Glaude, Jr. Chair of the Department of African American Studies at	*Begin Again: James Baldwin's America and Its Urgent Lessons for Our Own* (2020) ISBN 978-0-5255-7534-4 *Democracy in Black: How Race Still Enslaves the American Soul* (2016) ISBN 978-0-8041-3743-0

	Princeton University	https://www.youtube.com/watch?v=QKiB0APdxTo https://www.youtube.com/watch?v=qcLII_3IRxk https://www.youtube.com/watch?v=pgDB4ioX6Gk https://www.youtube.com/watch?v=caIHS1gkDjc https://www.youtube.com/watch?v=uuIFR5C6myM
9	Sarah Posner	*Unholy: Why White Evangelicals Worship at the Altar of Donald Trump* (2021) ISBN 978-1-9848-2042-6
10	Frank Schaeffer	*Crazy For God* (2007) ISBN 978-0-306-81750-2
11	Bishop Ithiel C. Clemmons, D.D.	*Bishop C. H. Mason and the Roots of the Church of God in Christ* (1996) ISBN 978-1-56229-451-9
12	Obery M. Hendricks, Jr.	*The Politics of Jesus: Rediscovering the True Revolutionary Nature of the Teaching of Jesus and How They Have Been Corrupted* (2006) ISBN 978-0-385-51665-5 *Christians Against Christianity: How Right-Wing Evangelicals Are Destroying Our Nation and Our Faith* (2021) ISBN 978-0-80705-740-7
13	*Shayne Looper, Pastor of Lockwood Community Church in Branch County*	https://www.yahoo.com/news/watch-christian-nationalism-051806037.html

14	Gregory A. Boyd	*The Myth of a Christian Nation: How the Quest for Political Power Is Destroying the Church* (2006) ISBN 0-310-26730-7
15	Andrew Greeley and Michael Hout	*The Truth About Conservative Christians* (2006) ISBN 978-0-226-30662-9
16	Video by Phil Vischer explaining the history of white conservative Christians in America.	https://fb.watch/5Brh3_tbOJ/2020
17	History of Pentecostalism in America	https://www.youtube.com/watch?v=EYqcSLhJESA - Church Splits - COGIC and Assemblies of God
18	Pastor Tony Evans, Oakcliff Bible Fellowship, Dallas, TX	https://www.youtube.com/watch?v=ao7sNItCkAY&list=RDLVao7sNItCkAY&index=1 https://www.youtube.com/watch?v=JmpD7SDkaDw&list=RDLVao7sNItCkAY&index=2
19	Rev. Dr. Martin Luther, Jr.	https://www.youtube.com/watch?v=7p5iOhXumaQ – MLK: Paul's Letter to American Christians https://www.youtube.com/watch?v=OOVaRxOy8ts – "Why Jesus Called a Man a Fool" https://www.youtube.com/watch?v=IMMxhjFYBgM - "Rise Up and Say, I am Somebody!" https://www.youtube.com/watch?v=GDRQTzNzu1I - "A Knock at Midnight" - February 11, 1962 (https://www.youtube.com/watch?v=1q881g1L_d8) – "The most segregated Hour in America"

20	Rev. Dr. Cheryl Sanders Professor of Christian Ethics Howard University School of Divinity, *Developing an Appetite for Justice*	https://www.youtube.com/watch?v=OLIvKqXqvJI&list=PLjJB0RTsdQsgEvBSqCjuVqtCF-8mLaog6&index=1
21	Jane Elliott on Her "Blue Eyes/Brown Eyes Exercise" and Fighting Racism https://janeelliott.com/	Jane Elliott on Her "Blue Eyes/Brown Eyes Exercise" and Fighting Racism - YouTube Jane Elliott's "Blue Eyes/Brown Eyes" Anti-Racism Exercise | The Oprah Winfrey Show | OWN - YouTube
22	Scott Reeder *Staff writer for* Illinois Times *Christian nationalism based on the misguided belief*	https://www.yahoo.com/news/scott-reeder-christian-nationalism-based-163120322.html
23	Paul D. Miller Professor of the practice of international affairs at Georgetown University and a research fellow with the Ethics and Religious Liberty Commission *What Is Christian Nationalism?*	https://www.christianitytoday.com/ct/2021/february-web-only/what-is-christian-nationalism.html

24	Fredrick Douglass *What to the Slave is the Fourth of July?*	https://americainclass.org/wp-content/uploads/2011/04/Douglass-FullText.pdf
25	David W. Heughins ("ProfDave") Adjunct Professor of History at Nazarene Bible College *Is Christianity Dangerous?*	https://www.thepostemail.com/2022/02/10/is-christianity-dangerous/
26	Rev. Jim Wallis American theologian, writer, teacher, and political activist. He is best known as the founder and editor of *Sojourners* magazine	https://www.youtube.com/watch?v=ZM95vlu_HwM
27	*He asked at Bible study if Black Lives Matter. Then, he says, Gateway Church kicked him out*	https://www.yahoo.com/news/asked-bible-study-black-lives-140000100.html
28	John Pavlovitz *White Evangelicals, This is Why People Are Through With You*	https://johnpavlovitz.com/2018/01/24/white-evangelicals-people/?fbclid=IwAR0YnNmAptZovfXMJAamUwvGA1wLPCi4dxYh-gyFCtQnSRnECN_mAY8pBEA
29	Russell Ellis *White Supremacy: Same Dog, Same*	https://www.youtube.com/watch?v=XUhbDZ4jwCQ

	Tricks-Time to Change the Training	
30	Patrick Smith *How some churches' ties to Trump-based politics are fueling an exodus of young evangelicals*	https://www.yahoo.com/news/why-one-evangelical-pastor-left-093340569.html
31	Christian Nationalism Is Infecting the United States	https://www.youtube.com/watch?v=Zi19gT8cJzA
32	Religious Extremists Mix Trump Worship With Christian Nationalism	https://www.youtube.com/watch?v=zx8tsompfiM
33	MSNBC - Rachel Maddow Christian Nationalism's Racist Past Precludes Revival Except Among GOP's Trumpiest	https://www.youtube.com/watch?v=oKrjhaPI95Y&t=175s
34	MSNBC - Ayman Christian Nationalism Is On The Rise	https://www.youtube.com/watch?v=kht_3z3hrQs&t=62
35	The Right's Fight to Make America a Christian Nation | CBS Reports	https://www.youtube.com/watch?v=pNclacx5a_g

36	Book Talk: Why White Evangelicals Support Trump Dr. Eddie Glaude, Jr. and Sarah Posner	https://www.youtube.com/watch?v=6ZQmSN1JEJ4
37	Kristin Du Mez: How White Evangelicals Corrupted a Faith and Fractured a Nation	Kristin Du Mez: How White Evangelicals Corrupted a Faith and Fractured a Nation - YouTube
38	Dr. Curtis Dodson, Chancellor of The Word Wise Institute of Eschatology	https://www.wordwiseinstitute.com/
39	Catherine Rampell, Washington Post, "Founding Fathers, Trashing Immigrants"	https://www.washingtonpost.com/opinions/from-benjamin-franklin-to-trump-the-history-of-americas-nativist-streak/2015/08/27/d41f9f26-4cf9-11e5-84df-923b3ef1a64b_story.html
40	Thomas Jefferson, 3rd US President, Founding Father	https://www.monticello.org/thomas-jefferson/jefferson-slavery/
41	Marvin Gaye – What's Going On	https://www.youtube.com/watch?v=H-kA3UtBj4M
42	Gerald L. K. Smith	https://en.wikipedia.org/wiki/Gerald_L._K._Smith
43	Murder of David Gunn	https://en.wikipedia.org/wiki/Murder_of_David_Gunn

Made in the USA
Middletown, DE
10 November 2024

63885115R00060